Nightmare at Scapa Flow

THE TRUTH ABOUT THE SINKING OF HMS *ROYAL OAK*

Nightmare at Scapa Flow

THE TRUTH ABOUT THE SINKING OF
HMS *ROYAL OAK*

H.J. WEAVER

BIRLINN

This edition first published in 2008 by
Birlinn Limited
West Newington House
10 Newington Road
Edinburgh
EH9 1QS

www.birlinn.co.uk

Reprinted 2013, 2015

First published in 1980 by Cressrelles Publishing Company Limited, Malvern

ISBN 978 1 84341 042 3

British Library Cataloguing-in-Publication Data
A catalogue record for this book is available from the British Library

Typeset by Iolaire Typesetting, Newtonmore
Printed and bound by Clays Ltd,
St Ives plc, Bungay Suffolk

Dedication

The battleship HMS *Royal Oak* was lost in Scapa Flow, the 'impregnable' main anchorage of the Home Fleet, on the night of October 13–14, 1939. Each year, on the Saturday closest to that date, surviving members of the crew gather before the war memorial at Southsea to pay tribute to the 833 officers and men who went down with their ship or died in the inhospitable waters of the Flow. No chaplain was present at the first service of remembrance I attended, and 'Taffy' Davies, a Royal Marine corporal at the time of the sinking, stepped with quiet dignity into the role of what he called 'the sin bo'sun'. The usual brief silence was observed, and he asked everyone to remember not only former shipmates, but 'sailors of every nation who fought and died for a cause they believed to be just'.

To those same men I dedicate this book.

H.J. WEAVER
January 1980

Facts do not cease to exist because they are ignored –

Contents

Illustrations

The *U-47* sailing from a French port

HMS *Royal Oak* during the First World War at full speed showing her guns at full elevation

Construction of the Churchill Barriers

HMS *Royal Oak* at anchor in Scapa Flow in 1939

The *U-47*

Buoy that marks the wreck of HMS *Royal Oak* and the grave of her crew

Günther Prien and Oberleutnant Hans Wessel receiving congratulations from the builders of *U-47*

Günther Prien being greeted by Vice Admiral Dönitz on 13 December 1939

Günther Prien being honoured by Hitler, October 1939

Part of one of the torpedoes which hit HMS *Royal Oak*

Glossary

In order to keep things as simple as possible, distances are given in yards and land miles, which everyone understands, rather than sea miles. It has not been possible, however, to avoid nautical terminology altogether, and this very brief glossary may be helpful to some readers. The prefix HMS is used for the first mention of each naval vessel.

Port   The left-hand side of a ship, looking towards the bow.

Starboard   The right-hand side of a ship, looking towards the bow.

Latitude   Position north or south of the equator, given in degrees, minutes and, sometimes, seconds ($55°06'18''N$). One degree equals 60 miles (69.09 land miles). There are 60 minutes in a degree, 60 seconds in a minute.

Longitude   Position east or west of Greenwich. One degree equals 60 sea miles at the equator but diminishes as you travel north or south.

Knot   One sea mile per hour (equivalent to 1.151 m.p.h.).

Bearing   The relation of a ship to another ship, or to one or more fixed points on land. The compass is divided into 360 degrees. North is $0°$ or $360°$; east, $90°$; south, $180°$; west $270°$.

ACOS   Admiral Commanding Orkneys and Shetlands.

PWSS   Port Wireless and Signal Station.

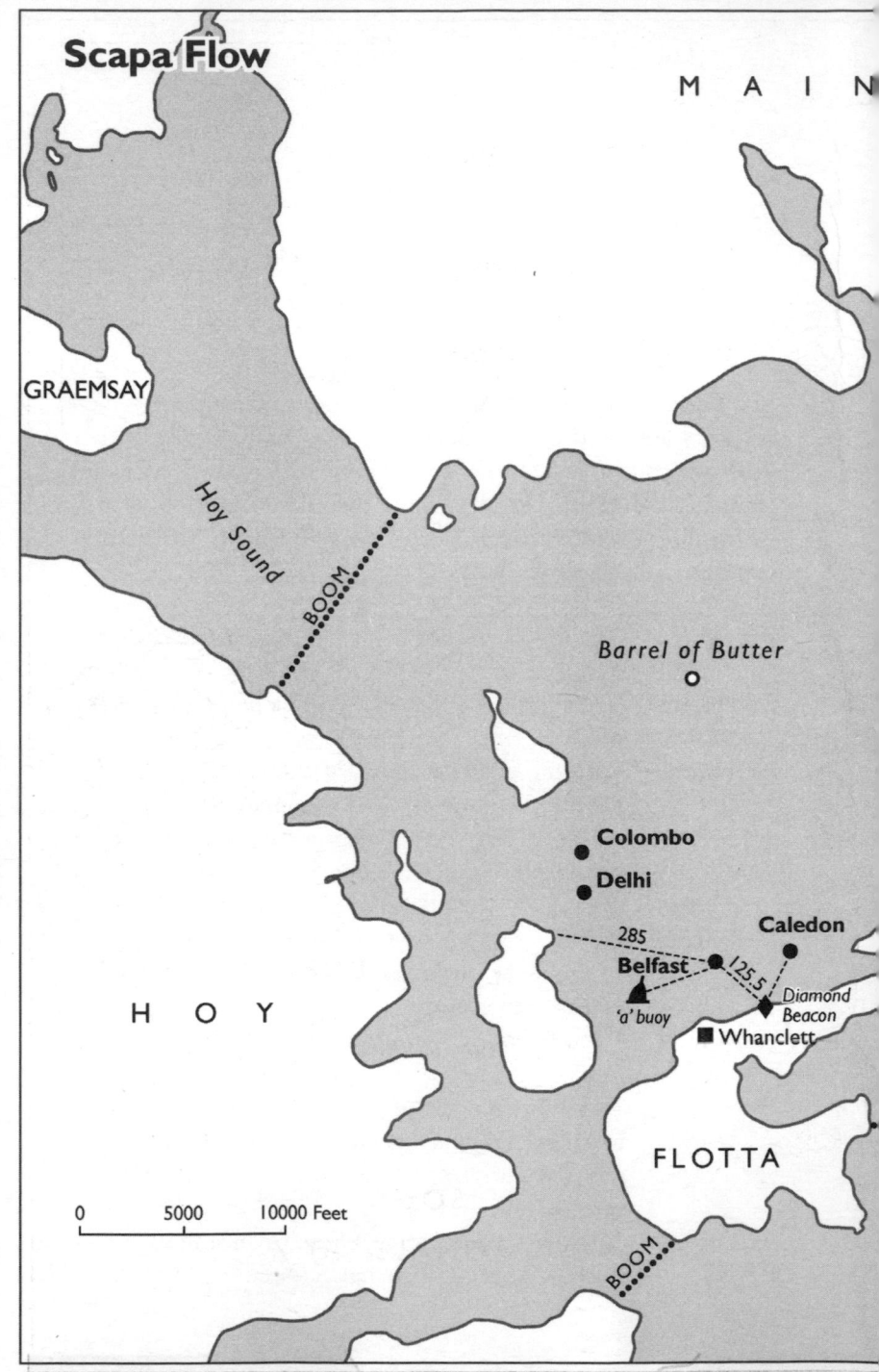

Scapa Flow

MAIN

GRAEMSAY

Hoy Sound

BOOM

Barrel of Butter

Colombo

Delhi

Caledon

285

Belfast

125.5

Diamond
Beacon

'a' buoy

Whanclett

H O Y

FLOTTA

0   5000   10000 Feet

BOOM

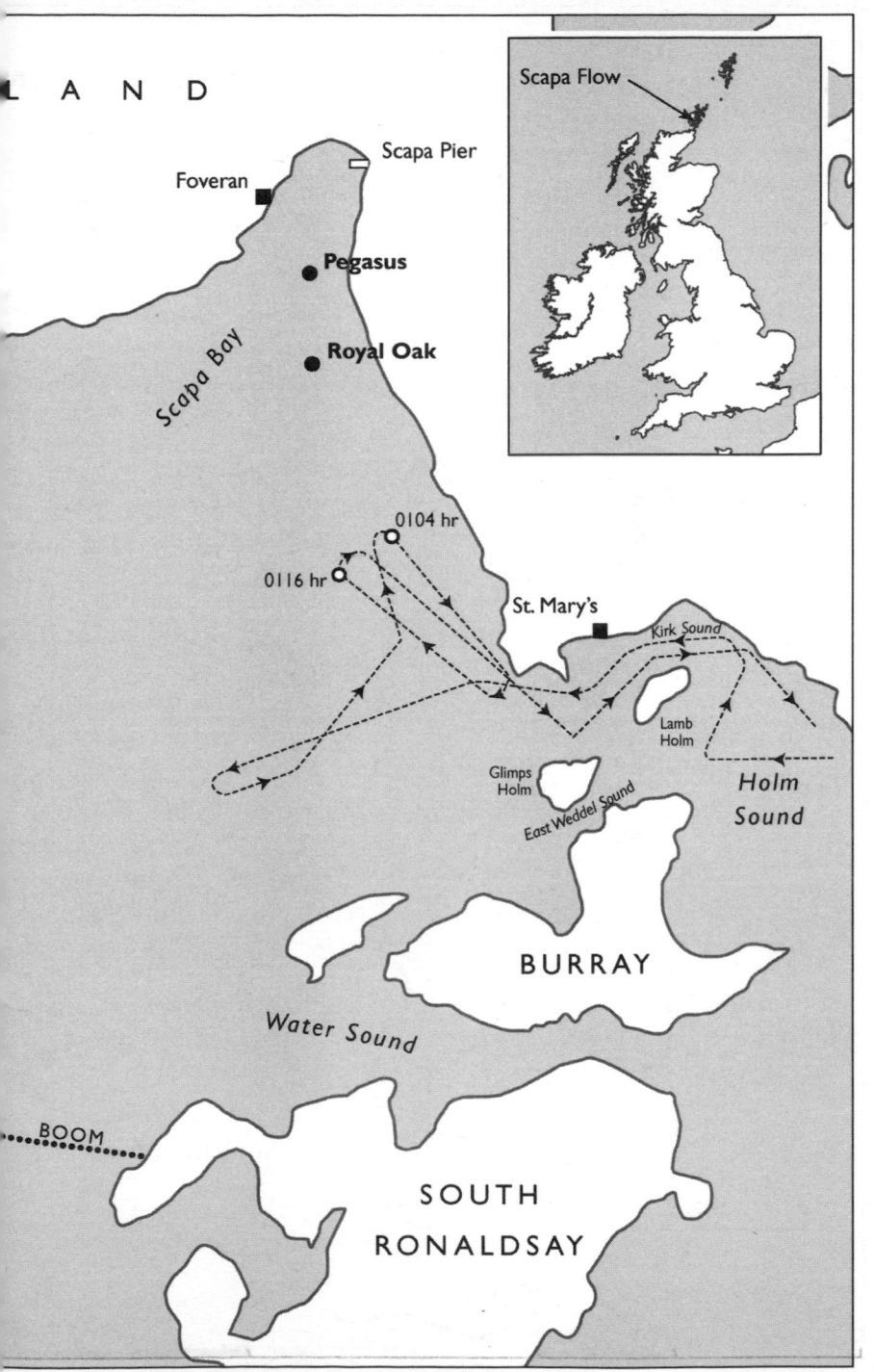

1

The Roots of Controversy

No naval incident of the last war has caused such a complex and enduring controversy as the sinking of HMS *Royal Oak*. The event has been dealt with in official and unofficial histories of the war at sea, it has been the subject of dozens of newspaper and magazine articles; and it has inspired one novel and three investigative books, the most recent of which appeared in 1976. All of these accounts are incomplete, inaccurate or contradictory – and frequently all three – with the result that, after 40 years and several million words, exactly what happened in Scapa Flow on that disastrous night for Britain is still far from clear.

It is the normal practice for writers lacking any formal qualifications in naval or historical matters to nod in the direction of their betters at about this point and acknowledge that 'no serious historian doubts that *Royal Oak* was torpedoed by the German submarine *U-47*, commanded by Kapitänleutnant Günther Prien'. However, if facts are the raw material of history, it is extraordinary how many facts historians have failed to provide about what is recognised as one of the great submarine exploits of all time. It is possible to read everything published to date about this spectacular feat of arms without being able to give a precise answer to any of the following basic questions:

- What ships of the Royal Navy were in Scapa Flow on the night *Royal Oak* was lost?
- Lt. Prien says in his log, or war diary, that the main Fleet anchorage was empty. Is this unlikely statement true? If not, what ships were there?

- When did the hunt for a suspected U-boat begin . . . what ships took part . . . when were the first depth charges dropped?
- One of the reasons given by Lt. Prien for making his escape from Scapa Flow after sinking *Royal Oak* is that he thought he had been seen by the driver of a car which stopped opposite him on the shore. Assuming that there was a car on the shore, who was the driver . . . where was he going . . . did he see the U-boat . . . why has he never come forward?
- According to Wilhelm Spahr, navigator of *U-47*, crew members on the submarine's bridge saw three guards on the shore as well as a car. Assuming this statement to be correct, who were these guards . . . what were they doing . . . why did they not see the U-boat?
- Lt. Prien also claimed to have torpedoed a twin-funnelled 'northern ship', subsequently named as the battlecruiser HMS *Repulse*, anchored some 600 yards beyond *Royal Oak*. The official British version of events is that *Repulse* was not in Scapa Flow at the time and Lt. Prien mistook the elderly, and comparatively tiny, sea-plane carrier HMS *Pegasus* for the battlecruiser. Where precisely was *Pegasus* anchored in relation to *Royal Oak*?
- In the light of what can be deduced about visibility in Scapa Flow on the night in question, is it likely that Lt. Prien saw *Pegasus* at all?
- According to the crew of *U-47*, part of the Scapa Flow defences reacted as if *Royal Oak* had been bombed, not torpedoed, and searchlights criss-crossed the sky above the U-boat. Was there an air raid alarm in Scapa Flow . . . how many land-based searchlights were in position . . . what action was taken by their crews?
- One version of the *U-47* story claims that the submarine, having escaped from Scapa Flow, was subjected to an attack by an armada of Royal Navy destroyers and patrol boats

from dawn to dusk on October 14. Which British warships were involved in this action, assuming that it took place?

- According to another version of the *U-47* story, this attack took place on October 15, not October 14. Assuming that this is the correct date, which British warships were involved?
- Who was blamed officially for the loss of *Royal Oak*?
- Was the blame justified?

It is the lack of firm answers to questions such as these which has ensured the continuation of the *Royal Oak* controversy for 40 years. The roots of the controversy are embedded in the fact that nobody has yet succeeded in reconciling Lt. Prien's story with the story told by the *Royal Oak* survivors, who, in the forthright manner of men of the sea, say that the German version of events is largely 'a load of old cobblers'.

'Taffy' Davies, the former Royal Marine corporal mentioned in the dedication to this book, is considered one of the most reliable *Royal Oak* witnesses, having escaped from the ship fully clothed and without even getting his feet wet, and he is today on terms of personal friendship with some ex-members of *U-47*'s crew. Yet the first time I met him he said: 'Sinking the old gal when we all thought we were safe inside Scapa Flow was an exploit of which the German Navy could be proud. Why didn't they leave it at that? Why all the inventions?

'The only way to avoid the conclusion that Lt. Prien was a complete and utter bloody liar is by saying Dr Goebbels put words into his mouth to make a better story for the German people – and, even if that was the case, he must have connived at it, which is not what you might expect of a German naval officer.' Mr Davies is also convinced that the only reason why the Admiralty has never officially denied Lt. Prien's story is 'because it shows the Admiralty in a much better light than the truth does'.

Naval historians shrug aside these objections with the explanation that 'Lt. Prien may have made a few mistakes in the course of a difficult night operation'. The *Royal Oak* survivors reply that this is rubbish and the inaccurate statements in the German story cannot be explained away as a few understandable errors in the dark. Even after all these years some of them still maintain that Lt. Prien's account is at such variance with the truth that there can be only one explanation: he never saw the inside of Scapa Flow and their ship was either torpedoed by another U-boat commander, or blew up accidentally, or was blown up by a saboteur.

The situation is complicated by the fact that what might now be called the German story is made up of several strands. First there is Lt. Prien's log. Then there is the war diary of Grand Admiral Karl Dönitz, who (as Commodore Dönitz) was in charge of the U-boat war in 1939. This gives details of radio reports from *U-47* and Lt. Prien's personal report on his safe return to Germany.

Furthermore, some unofficial sources exist. Lt. Prien made a broadcast from Berlin about his exploit. A number of newspaper stories also appeared, based on interviews with him and his crew. These were followed in 1940 by an autobiography, *Mein Weg Nach Scapa Flow*, which was published in English after the war. In addition, his crew have added various elements in post-war interviews, including the three guards on the shore, the searchlights in the sky, and the attack on *U-47* on either October 14 or 15.

One of four typed copies of Lt. Prien's log, together with an accompanying map which shows the course taken by *U-47* inside Scapa Flow, was captured at the end of the war. The log, with two different translations, is now held at Greenwich Maritime Museum. There seems no reason to doubt its authenticity. A document attached to it shows that it was examined by several German planning officers in March, 1942, when an aerial torpedo attack on Scapa Flow was under consideration.

The log describes how Lt. Prien slipped into the Flow

through Kirk Sound, one of the four narrow eastern entrances, shortly after midnight, having negotiated a northerly course on the surface around the blockships which were supposed to make the passage impossible. By 0027 hours, still on the surface, he was heading westwards across the Flow towards the main Fleet anchorage. It was so bright that he could see from a range of 9,000 yards that the anchorage was empty. He also feared that *U-47* was about to expose herself to detection by the guard at Hoxa Sound, one of the Flow's southern entrances, which was protected by a boom. *U-47* went about and made for the northeast corner of the Flow.

Here, at last, Lt. Prien found two 'fat fellows'. A pencilled note in the margin identifies them as *Repulse* and *Royal Oak*. In the first attack, one torpedo struck the starboard bow of *Repulse*. Lt. Prien stood off, reloaded and returned for a second attack with a salvo of three torpedoes on *Royal Oak*. All three torpedoes struck their target, there was a spectacular explosion, and Lt. Prien decided to make his escape, partly because he feared he had been seen by the driver of the car on the shore, partly because – as one would expect in the ordinary course of events – the anchorage had 'sprung to life'.

Back in Kirk Sound, he took the gap to the south of the blockships. The tide was now falling and he had to battle *against* a fierce 10-knot current. Nevertheless, by 0215 the U-boat had regained the comparative safety of the open sea. By dawn, when she submerged, *U-47* had crossed the Moray Firth. From there the U-boat made her way home largely as she had come, proceeding by night, lying hidden by day, and eventually reached Wilhelmshaven on the morning of Tuesday, October 17. Later, Lt. Prien and his crew were flown to Kiel, then to Berlin, where they received a heroes' welcome and a personal audience with the Führer.

According to Admiral Dönitz, *U-47* sent a radio message on October 15 saying that *Royal Oak* had been sunk and *Repulse* damaged, and, on reaching Wilhelmshaven, Lt. Prien repeated these claims. His subsequent broadcast and the newspaper accounts which appeared next morning added some minor details. The really dramatic version of his story, however, is contained in *Mein Weg Nach Scapa Flow*, given the title *I Sank The Royal Oak* when it was published in Britain in 1954.

After dealing with the first attack, in which *Repulse* was damaged, this is how it describes the last moments of *Royal Oak:* 'A wall of water shot up towards the sky. It was as if the sea suddenly stood up on end. Loud explosions came one after another like drumfire in a battle and coalesced into one mightily ear-splitting crash. Flames shot skyward, blue . . . yellow . . . red. Behind this hellish firework display the sky disappeared entirely. Like huge birds, black shadows soared through the flames, fell hissing and splashing into the water. Fountains yards high sprang up where they had fallen, huge fragments of the mast and funnels. We must have hit the munition magazine and the deadly cargo had torn the body of its own ship apart. It was as if the gates of hell had suddenly been torn open and I was looking into the flaming furnace . . .'

Lt. Prien then goes on to describe how the harbour 'awoke to feverish activity. Searchlights flashed and probed with their long white fingers over the water and died. Lights were flitting here and there . . . small swift lights low over the water, the lights of destroyers and U-boat chasers. Like dragonflies they zig-zagged over the dark surface. If they caught us we were done for . . .'

Then, as *U-47* struggled against the fierce current in Kirk Sound, 'the headlight [*sic*] of a destroyer detached itself from the welter of light and came streaking towards us . . . It was a nightmare. There we lay, held fast by an invisible power, while death came closer, ever closer. A spot of light flashed dot-dash-dot. "He is signalling," whispered Endrass [note: one of *U-47*'s two watch officers]. The boat shuddered as it strained against the current. We must get out . . . *we must get out* . . . Then – wonder of wonders – the pursuer turned aside. The light slid away over the water and then came the *weeyum* of the first depth charges.'

It is Lt. Prien's story which the world has accepted. But the *Royal Oak* survivors maintain that it is false in most major respects: it was a dark night, not a bright night; *Repulse* had left Scapa Flow and the only ship anywhere near *Royal Oak* was *Pegasus*; the end of *Royal Oak* was quiet, not spectacular; and Scapa Flow did not spring to life but remained gloomy and silent while they struggled for their lives in the chill October sea.*

In the course of various attempts to reconcile these two opposing versions of the exploit, there is hardly a detail, no matter how small, that has not been mulled over and argued about. For everyone prepared to say one thing, it is usually possible to find someone prepared to say exactly the opposite, even when the point at issue can easily be settled by simple research.

The car on the shore has become a car with one blazing headlamp, a car with two blazing headlamps, a truck with two blazing headlamps and a man on a bicycle, and the incident is supposed to have occurred as *U-47* passed the village of St Mary's on the shores of Kirk Sound during the penetration of Scapa Flow; immediately after the salvo of three torpedoes struck *Royal Oak* (although *U-47* was nearly two miles from the nearest road at the time); and as *U-47* passed St Mary's on her way *out* of Scapa Flow.

Debates about visibility include confident assertions that there was a big, bright moon and no moon at all, brilliant Northern Lights, intermittent Northern Lights and no Northern Lights. It has been said that Lt. Prien torpedoed no other ship except *Royal Oak*. Alternatively it has been argued

---

* The *Royal Oak* survivors have not been entirely without German support for their story. Walter Schellenberg, who served for many years in SS Foreign Intelligence, ultimately became its chief and was appointed head of the unified German secret services after the arrest of Admiral Wilhelm Canaris in 1944, says in his memoirs that Lt. Prien 'was already on his way back to the open sea before the British even knew what was happening'.

that, in addition to *Royal Oak*, he torpedoed *Pegasus*, the twin-funnelled battlecruiser HMS *Hood*, the twin-funnelled battlecruiser HMS *Renown*,* or the twin-funnelled and partly demilitarised battleship HMS *Iron Duke*, which served as the headquarters of Admiral Sir Wilfred French, Admiral Commanding, Orkneys and Shetlands (ACOS).

At the time of the attack it has been said that the bows of *Royal Oak* were pointing north-east, south-east, south, east and north, the last heading leading one writer to the interesting conclusion that Lt. Prien must have fired his torpedoes from a point one and a half miles inland; and the relative position of *Pegasus* has been given as half a mile (or up to two miles) to the north (or maybe north-west, west or south-west) of *Royal Oak*.

Most of this confusion might have been dispelled with the publication in 1976 of *The Royal Oak Disaster* by Gerald S. Snyder, an American who set out to tell 'the full story . . . from both sides' with 'no axe to grind, no particular case to argue'. Mr Snyder had the advantage of access to a vital piece which had always been missing from the jigsaw – the Admiralty documents, released for public scrutiny in 1971 when the 50-year secrecy embargo was reduced to 30 years.

Unfortunately, he appears to have ignored nearly all of these documents and concentrated for the British version of events in Scapa Flow almost entirely on the evidence given to the *Royal Oak* Board of Inquiry and the Board's findings. It is not possible to tell the 'full story' if you rely mainly on these two sources. The Board did not deal at all with certain aspects of the exploit (what ships of the Royal Navy were in Scapa Flow at the time, for example); the evidence was frequently general rather than specific (there is no indication of the precise time at which a hunt for a suspected U-boat began, what ships were involved, when the first depth charges were dropped); and the evidence

---

* With the exception of *Renown*, the whereabouts of these ships is given elsewhere in the text. *Renown* sailed from Scapa Flow on Oct. 2 and arrived at Freetown, Sierra Leone, at 0723/Oct. 12.

was not always accurate (the Admiralty, having lost *Royal Oak*, proceeded to mislay the wreck: it is not in the position indicated in the Board of Inquiry files).

Consequently, *The Royal Oak Disaster* gives no answer, or the wrong answer, to the questions at the beginning of this chapter. It also contains a number of serious inconsistencies and, in some respects, manages to add to, rather than dispel, the confusion which surrounds the exploit. No useful purpose would be served by an exhaustive analysis of the book, but the following points illustrate the validity of these criticisms.

Of Lt. Prien's autobiography, *The Royal Oak Disaster* says that 'as a general chronicle of the major – and minor – events as they relate to Prien and his Scapa Flow mission, it can be relied upon.' These major and minor events include presumably the destroyers and U-boat chasers hunting for a submarine immediately after the second attack on *Royal Oak*, the challenge by a destroyer which mysteriously turned aside, and the *weeyum* of the first depth charges as *U-47* finally made her escape. Elsewhere, however, Mr Snyder says: 'Admiral French did send his destroyers out. But by the time they arrived *Royal Oak* was gone, *U-47* had made her exit - never was there a race between *U-47* and her pursuers, not a depth charge was dropped on *U-47* . . .'

The text of *The Royal Oak Disaster* describes how the car on the shore was seen as *U-47* passed St Mary's on her way into Scapa Flow. However, the book also reproduces a map, drawn by Wilhelm Spahr, *U-47*'s navigator, which indicates that the car and the three guards were seen as *U-47* was *leaving* Scapa Flow.*

---

* The unsatisfactory state of knowledge about Lt. Prien's mission is indicated by the fact that publishers, too, frequently print contradictory versions of the same episode without any attempt to discover which, if either, is true. A paperback edition of *Enemy Submarine* by Wolfgang Frank, who served on Admiral Dönitz's staff during the war, appeared in Britain in 1977. Herr Frank repeats the claim that *Repulse* was torpedoed in Scapa Flow. The British publishers, however, have interpolated in the text the official British story that Lt. Prien mistook *Pegasus* for the battlecruiser.

Lt. Prien stated in his log that, although the tide was falling, he had to fight his way out of Scapa Flow against a 10-knot current. The *Royal Oak* Board of Inquiry made the point that, if he had escaped immediately after the attack which sank the battleship, the force of the current against him would have been 'perhaps as much as eight knots'. But according to *The Royal Oak Disaster* both Lt. Prien and the Board were mistaken: '. . . he had the current, he didn't have to fight it – the Tide Tables for the night of 13 October show he had a strong outgoing tide . . .' It is not possible, however, to deduce from tide tables the flow of currents in complicated channels like the Orkneys.

The Royal Oak Disaster also says it is 'surprising . . . in view of the proof of negligence contained in the records . . . that no one in the Navy received so much as a reprimand for one of the worst disasters in its history'. This is not the case. A well-respected and well-liked officer was placed on the retired list, quite harshly and unjustly, over the loss of *Royal Oak*.

One of the difficulties in writing about Lt. Prien is that he gave his life for his country when *U-47*, with a somewhat changed crew, was sunk by the destroyer HMS *Wolverine* on March 8, 1941.* As a result, any suggestion that a statement made by him, or supposed to have been made by him, is less than accurate tends to be regarded as an unwarranted attack on a dead man who cannot answer for himself. This book was never envisaged as an attack on, or defence of, Lt. Prien. It began – although that is not where it ended – as an attempt to establish, after the passage of nearly four decades, the facts about the night on which *Royal Oak* was lost.

The simplest way is to tell the story as it happened.

---

* Lt. Prien's two watch officers, Lt. Englebert Endrass and Lt. Amelung von Varendorff, who were on *U-47*'s bridge during the *Royal Oak* action, also failed to survive the war. Both were lost after being given their own commands.

2

Wrong-way Charlie

Lt. Prien sailed from Kiel on the sunny morning of October 8, the sixth Sunday of the war, to fulfil an old dream of the German Navy, an attack on ships of the Home Fleet while their crews thought themselves safe in an enemy-proof anchorage.

For 19-year-old Leading Seaman Herbert Herrmann, one of *U-47*'s torpedo mechanics who now lives in a council house on the shores of the Solway Firth and works for ICI as an engineer, it was his first mission, and, once he heard where he was going, he felt fairly confident that it would be his last.* 'There are about 15 of us left now from the 1939 crew of *U-47* and we often disagree when we talk about the trip', he told me at his home in his soft Borders accent. 'Some remember one thing, some another. But it's not true that the skipper revealed where we were going just before we went in. He told us the first time we were bedded down on the bottom of the North Sea, and he added that we needn't make the trip if we didn't want to.' He laughed, which is something he does readily. 'It wasn't much of an offer when we were already at sea.'

* Mr Herrmann's career as a submariner ended abruptly in 1944 when *U-1209* ran herself onto some rocks, topped by a lighthouse, off the coast of Cornwall. He was taken prisoner and decided to make his life in Britain after the war. The somewhat undistinguished end to his career at sea was the result, he says, of 'a simple error of navigation', but he takes the philosophical view that it was 'better than being brought up on the end of a fish hook'.

In addition, Lt. Prien gave his crew the depressing news, according to Mr Herrmann, that 'everyone had more or less given up hope of our coming back alive'. That was not an unreasonable assumption: two similar missions in the first World War had ended in disaster. However, Lt. Prien made it clear that he did not share the pessimism at U-boat head-quarters. He said confidently: 'I'm determined to get you in there, do what they want me to do and get you out again.'

The mission had been planned in person by Commodore Dönitz. In his memoirs he reveals that he looked upon it as 'the boldest of bold enterprises' and that he worked in the belief 'that the entrances to Scapa, the most important of all British Fleet anchorages, would be so well protected by nets, minefields, booms, guardships and patrols that the Admiralty, with all its great experience in these matters, and the Commander-in-Chief of the Home Fleet, must have complete confidence in the effectiveness of the measures taken and felt quite sure that the British warships were perfectly secure in their anchorage'.

At the time there were seven recognised entrances to Scapa Flow. To the east an approach through Holm Sound gave access to three entrances, Kirk, Skerry and East Weddel Sounds, and there was another separate entrance, Water Sound. To the south were two entrances, Hoxa and Switha Sounds, both guarded by booms, and to the north-west Hoy Sound, also guarded by a boom.

In the first World War the Admiralty had relied upon blockships to seal the eastern entrances. This policy had created such fierce currents that in the years of peace, and of neglect, some blockships had partially disintegrated or shifted from their original positions. Despite being warned of the dangers, the Admiralty had adopted a vacillating attitude towards strength-ening the defences of the eastern entrances. Another blockship, the *Soriano*, had been sunk in Kirk Sound on March 15, 1939, followed by the *Cape Ortegal* in the adjoining Skerry Sound on

September 8, 1939. Nevertheless, none of the four eastern entrances was completely sealed and the Admiralty relied mainly on the speed of the currents, which ran one way or the other for most of the day at up to 10 knots, to protect Scapa Flow against penetration by a U-boat.

By September 26, largely on the basis of aerial reconnaissance, Commodore Dönitz had come to the conclusion that Kirk Sound was vulnerable to a submarine of *U-47*'s type, capable of 17 knots on the surface. In the *U-Boat Command War Diary* he noted that it appeared to be blocked 'by two merchant ships, apparently sunk across the channel of Kirk Sound, and by another a little more to the north. South of them, up to Lamb Holm, there exists a gap 550 feet wide with a depth of water of $22\frac{3}{4}$ feet up to the shallows. North of these wrecks there is also a gap, but narrower. On the two shores the coast is almost uninhabited. Here I think it would certainly be possible to penetrate – by night, on the surface, at slack water. The main difficulties will be navigational.'

The ideal date had an air of Wagnerian doom about it – Friday, October 13. There would be one of the highest tides of the year; high water, and the slacks on either side of it that night, would be at a time when most people could be expected to have retired to bed; and the moon would not only be new, but rise and set in the hours of daylight.

All that remained was to select the right man for the task. He chose Lt. Prien: 'He, in my opinion, possessed all the personal qualities and professional ability required. I handed over to him the whole file on the subject and left him free to accept the task or not, as he saw fit. I added that I wanted him to think it over for at least 48 hours before giving me his answer.'

Lt. Prien was 30, the son of a judge. After qualifying as a merchant navy officer, he accepted a German Navy commission when Hitler came to power and, a few months before the outbreak of war, was given his first and only command, *U-47*. September 3, 1939, had found him conveniently placed in the Bay of Biscay, near the main shipping lanes, and he was rewarded with three quick successes, all British – the merchant ships *Bosnia* (2,407 tons, September 5), *Rio Claro* (4,086 tons, September 6) and *Gartavon* (1,777 tons, September 7). *U-47* arrived back in Kiel on September 15 and was being made ready for her next patrol when Lt. Prien was given the opportunity to undertake, or refuse, the Scapa Flow mission. He willingly accepted the challenge.

According to Lt. Prien, Commodore Dönitz asked him if he had considered all the facts carefully, not to mention the fate of the two commanders, von Hennig (captured) and Emsmann (killed), who had failed to return from similar missions in the first World War. Lt. Prien replied that he had. 'Very well, get your boat ready,' said Commodore Dönitz. 'We will fix the time of departure later.' He walked round from behind his desk and the two men shook hands.

And then the German Navy proceeded to mount a separate operation whose ultimate effect was to sabotage *U-47*'s mission and rob Lt. Prien of far more important targets than the venerable *Royal Oak*. Twenty-four hours before *U-47* sailed to attack the Home Fleet inside Scapa Flow, the battlecruiser *Gneisenau*, the cruiser *Köln* and an escort force of nine destroyers were despatched north to the Utshire Light, off the south-west coast of Norway, to lure the Home Fleet *out* of Scapa Flow.

This foray had two purposes. It was meant to divert attention from two German pocket battleships, *Graf Spee* and *Deutschland*, operating in the Atlantic. In addition, if the Home Fleet accepted the bait, they were to be received on the other side of the North Sea by a welcoming force of 127 Heinkels, 21 Ju88 dive-bombers and four U-boats.

Initially, the plan worked perfectly. *Gneisenau* and the rest of the German force were spotted by a Hudson of RAF Coastal Command. At the Admiralty it was assumed that the German battlecruiser was making an attempt to break out into the Atlantic.

On Sunday, October 8, as *U-47* emerged from the Kiel Canal and set course for the Orkneys, the Humber Force sailed from Rosyth and the Home Fleet from Scapa Flow – the battle-cruisers HMS *Hood* and *Repulse*, the battleships HMS *Nelson* and HMS *Rodney*, the aircraft carrier HMS *Furious*, the cruisers HMS *Aurora*, HMS *Sheffield* and HMS *Newcastle* and their escorts. *Nelson* flew the flag of Admiral Sir Charles Forbes, C.-in-C. of the Home Fleet, already known, rather unkindly, to the lower deck as 'Wrong-way Charlie' because of his failure to make contact with any units of the German Fleet in six weeks of war.

Behind the main force wallowed *Royal Oak*, an old ship with a smart crew but few memories, too slow now even to keep station when the Fleet was at sea and not expected to survive the scrapyard for long. In the action that might lie ahead she had been cast very much in the role of an outfielder and sent with an escort of two destroyers to patrol the Fair Isle channel.

Royal Oak had been built at Devonport in the first World War at a cost of £2.5 million and commissioned in May, 1916. On May 31 she took part in the Battle of Jutland, fired seven salvoes at 14,000 yards and was credited with two hits. Her other main claim to distinction was to have been the setting for a sequence of events which led to rumours of mutiny in the Mediterranean Fleet, two of the Royal Navy's more memorable courts-martial, the dismissal of a Rear-Admiral, international headlines, confident predictions that the collapse of the British Empire could not be far away – and, for newspaper readers, a rare glimpse of the inner workings of the Silent Service, the old Royal Navy, the same Royal Navy which sailed to keep the seas in 1939.

It all began in the Grand Harbour at Malta on the eve of another Friday the 13th – January 13, 1928 – when, it was said, Rear-Admiral Bernard St George Collard called Bandmaster Barnacle of the Royal Marines 'a bugger'. (See Appendix C.)

*

During that second week of October, 1939, the weather was terrible. In *U-47*, Herbert Herrmann spent most of his nights, when the U-boat surfaced, being violently seasick. Conditions were, if anything, worse 400 miles to the north where *Royal Oak* was patrolling the Fair Isle channel. 'Taffy' Davies remembers it as 'one of the worst trips I've ever known at sea. Both batteries were awash and you couldn't have manned a 6-inch gun if your life depended on it.' Nearly all the life-saving Carley floats were smashed.

From everyone's point of view, the *Gneisenau* foray proved an almost total fiasco. A force of 12 Wellington bombers failed to locate the German ships, which slipped back through the Kattegat to Kiel. The German bombers failed to find the Home Fleet, made contact with the less important Humber Force, bombed it, but did not score a hit. The waiting U-boats did not enter into the action at all. On the afternoon of October 9, Admiral Forbes learned of the withdrawal of *Gneisenau* and ordered his own ships back to port.

The verdict on the lower deck was, naturally enough: 'Wrong-way Charlie has done it again'. But Admiral Forbes made one vital decision which was to have far-reaching consequences for the success of Lt. Prien's mission. Although the Humber Force returned to the Forth, he ordered the dispersal of the Home Fleet, a decision dictated largely by fears about the vulnerability of Scapa Flow to air attack.

He sent the battleships *Hood, Nelson* and *Rodney* to Loch Ewe on the west coast of Scotland, where they arrived on Wednesday, October 11. The cruiser *Sheffield* remained at sea. *Royal Oak*, the battlecruiser *Repulse*, the aircraft carrier *Furious*, the cruiser *Newcastle* and the Destroyer Command cruiser *Aurora* returned to Scapa Flow with their escorts, arriving at various times on October 11. First was *Royal Oak* at 0705 when she took up her usual station in the north-east corner of the Flow: she always anchored there so that her guns could be used to protect the RDF (later

Radar) station at Netherbutton in the event of an air attack.

But in his Report of Proceedings Admiral Forbes noted: *'Repulse* to Scapa, then Rosyth to dock.' Even that prize, far richer than *Royal Oak*, was to be removed beyond Lt. Prien's grasp.

3

The Car on the Shore

As *U-47* approached the Orkneys, an entirely false, but enduring, impression of the scene in Scapa Flow was being created
back in Germany. It is still part of the Lt. Prien legend that Fate
robbed him at the eleventh hour of far greater success than he
actually achieved. Two reconnaissance flights are said to have
caused a stampede of the Home Fleet out of Scapa Flow and left
the anchorage as empty as a ballroom after the band has gone
home.

This entirely inaccurate assessment of the situation stems
largely from an entry in the *U-Boat Command War Diary*, which
reads in part: '11th October. Without having received orders, an
aircraft of the 2nd Air Fleet flew over Scapa Flow at low
altitude. On the 12th October at 1500 hours an aircraft of
Group A (S/Lt Newe, with Warrant Officers Bohme and
Wolff) carried out an excellent reconnaissance which showed
the exact position of an aircraft carrier, five heavy ships and ten
cruisers. This reconnaissance was commented upon verbally
during the night by S/Lt Newe at Wilhelmshaven. A message
was sent to *U-47*, which did not receive it, for the submarine
was, at that moment, lying on the bottom . . .

'According to the observations of the listening service, a
large number of ships got under way. It is possible that they
did so because the appearance, on two occasions, of aircraft
above Scapa Flow made them begin to fear an attack on the
base. These nights would appear to have had a regrettable
result . . .'

The confidential *Pink List*, which gave the whereabouts of

ships of the Royal Navy at 1600 hours each day, checked against the logs of ships of the Home Fleet, shows that there were 63 naval vessels in Scapa Flow at the time of the reconnaissance flight on the Thursday afternoon. The largest and/or most important were the aircraft carrier *Furious, Repulse, Royal Oak*, and *Iron Duke*, moored at C buoy off Lyness naval base; three heavy cruisers *Newcastle*, HMS *Southampton* and HMS *Glasgow*); and five light cruisers (*Aurora*, HMS *Cardiff*, HMS *Caledon*, HMS *Calypso* and HMS *Dunedin*).*

Between the time of the aerial reconnaissance and dawn on the morning of Friday, October 13, nine naval vessels sailed from Scapa Flow. The first, as planned, was *Repulse* at 1734, to dock at Rosyth, accompanied by the destroyers *Fame* and *Foresight*.† As the belief still exists widely in Germany that *Repulse* was Lt. Prien's 'northern ship', it is worth giving the battle-cruiser's movements in some detail to put matters beyond doubt.

* The other vessels consisted of 13 destroyers (HMS *Somali*, HMS *Ashanti*, HMS *Mashona*, HMS *Matabele*, HMS *Tartar*, HMS *Eskimo*, HMS *Fearless*, HMS *Foxhound*, HMS *Fame*, HMS *Foresight*, HMS *Jervis*, HMS *Jupiter* and HMS *Sturdy* (attached to *Furious*); five minesweepers (HMS *Hazard*, HMS *Hebe*, HMS *Seagull*, HMS *Sharpshooter* and HMS *Speedy*); the A/A ship *Curlew*; the seaplane carrier *Pegasus*; 10 armed merchant cruisers (*Asturias, Aurania, Scotstoun, California, Chitral, Montclare, Rawalpindi, Salopian, Transylvania* and *Voltaire*, being used as an accommodation ship); the destroyer depot and repair ship *Greenwich*; the netlayer *Guardian*; the auxiliary minesweeping trawlers *Silicia* and *Sterton*; the Fleet tugs *Bandit* and *St Martin*; nine boom defence vessels (*Barbican, Barcroft, Barlow, Barranca, Brine, Dragonet, Moorgate, Plantagenet* and *Signet*); and six Fleet drifters (*Fumarole, Harmattan, Horizon, Indian Summer, Sheen* and *Shower*). In addition, the hospital snip *Aba* was in the anchorage. The two 'heavy ships' of the Home Fleet not at either Scapa Flow or Loch Ewe *were* HMS *Royal Sovereign* at Plymouth and HMS *Ramillies* (detached) at Gibraltar.
† The other six vessels were *Glasgow* (1737), *Dunedin* (1810) and *Newcastle* (1915), to patrol in the Atlantic with *Glasgow*; and *Furious* (0140), to Loch Ewe, escorted by the destroyers *Foxhound* and *Fearless*.

The log of *Southampton* contains the entry for October 12: '*Repulse* . . . to sea.' The battlecruiser's log shows that by 2249 on the Thursday night she had crossed the Moray Firth and was some 10 miles off Fraserburgh (Rattray Head 174°, Kinnaird's Head 210°). *Repulse* entered the Forth next morning, passed the boom defence at 0845, passed beneath the Forth Bridge at 0902, secured to No. 14 buoy at 0946, proceeded to Rosyth Dockyard at 1415 and entered dry dock at 1540. A start was made on pumping out the dock at 0900 on the Saturday morning and from 1300 hours hands were employed painting the ship's bottom. *Repulse* left dock on Tuesday, October 17, and sailed at 1233 on October 18 for Loch Ewe.

Ashore and afloat, Friday, October 13, passed much like any other day at Scapa Flow while *U-47* lay off the Orkneys, waiting for nightfall.

Ships came, ships went. The light cruisers HMS *Delhi* and HMS *Colombo* arrived early in the morning and joined *Caledon* and *Calypso* in the main Fleet anchorage (and almost certainly *Cardiff* as well, although *Cardiff*'s log does not give an anchor bearing). *Southampton* weighed anchor at 1016 and sailed to patrol off the Shetlands, escorted by *Matabele, Jervis* and *Jupiter*, plus the destroyers HMS *Jackal* and HMS *Janus*, which had arrived from Rosyth. *Sturdy* left for Rosyth at 1145. HMS *Belfast*, newest and largest cruiser in the Royal Navy, entered harbour at 1500 hours – the last-but-one ship movement of the day – and anchored at 1520 in the main Fleet anchorage, half a mile off the island of Flotta. Even now, James Sutherland, a farmer who lived in a house called Whanclett, slightly west of where *Belfast* let go her anchor, remembers her arrival. 'I could always tell the *Belfast* and the *Edinburgh* by the arrangement of their funnels,' he explained. 'The second mast was in front of the second funnel instead of being the other way around.'

On land, the war had already begun to swamp the Orkney

port of Kirkwall. At the Royal, the one hotel to escape requisitioning, residents slept on the floor and before one meal was finished long queues had begun to form outside the dining-room for the next. Like the staff at the Royal, Robbie Tullock, owner of a Kirkwall garage, was run off his feet. The demand for his big black Ford V8 taxi with the registration number BS 1654 was endless. Once again he could not see much prospect of getting to bed before midnight: events would prove him right.

Wrens had already appeared in Kirkwall at this time and made the depressing discovery that it was not exactly the Mayfair of the north. There was little in the way of amusement after working hours. But, as they went about their duties on that Friday, they had something to look forward to. There was to be a dance in the Drill Hall at St Mary's and a special bus had been arranged to take them down to the shores of Kirk Sound, six miles away.

Aboard *Royal Oak*, four Engine Room Artificers and a Canteen Assistant spent the afternoon packing their kit. Before the day was out they were due to make the journey across the Flow to the main Fleet anchorage, the ERAs to carry out repairs to the cruiser *Colombo*, the Canteen Assistant to join the crew of the cruiser *Delhi*. Some of *Royal Oak*'s crew went ashore for the afternoon. Among them was Chief ERA Wilson, who after pay parade had been seized by a sudden complusion to buy a torch. Less than 12 hours later it would help to save his life. One of Admiral French's cooks aboard *Iron Duke* went ashore as well. He would never cook another meal: after missing his liberty boat at Scapa Pier, he went to spend the night with a friend in *Royal Oak* and was lost.

For the crew of *U-47*, the time for patient waiting was over. The U-boat surfaced at 1915. Torpedoes had already been placed in rapid-loading positions, explosive charges made ready in case of the need to scuttle. Their cook had done them well – soup, salt pork and vegetables, a pudding and coffee – for a meal which seemed quite likely to be their last at sea until the war was over and quite possibly their last anywhere.

It was a fine clear night with light cloud behind which flickered the Northern Lights.* They were an unforeseen and unexpected hazard, but, although deprived of his promised cloak of total darkness, Lt. Prien decided it would be unfair to his keyed-up crew to postpone the mission for another 24 hours. Once supper was over, he set course for Rose Ness at the entrance to Holm Sound. From there he would have roughly three miles to cover before reaching the entrance to Kirk Sound, then the better part of another two miles before emerging into Scapa Flow. Kirk Sound posed the main threat to the success of the exploit, both in terms of detection and navigation: it was little more than 600 yards wide at its narrowest point and, apart from the four periods of slack water each day when the tide turned, the current ran like a mill race.

Timing of the approach was therefore critical and had to take into account the additional complication that slack water did not coincide with high water and low water. The main tidal flow in the Orkneys is between the Atlantic and the North Sea, and, in the days before the eastern entrances were sealed off with road-topped stone barriers, the sea flowed *into* Scapa Flow through the eastern entrances and *out* through the western entrances for most of the time that the tide was falling in the anchorage. The

---

* Despite all the arguments which have raged over visibility, there is no doubt that the Northern Lights were active that night. The log of *Southampton*, patrolling east of the Shetlands, some 175 miles away, contains the entry: '2030 Observed the Aurora Borealis.' This is confirmed by the log of *Jackal*, one of her escorting destroyers: 'An excellent display of Northern Lights throughout the watch.' John Laughton, an Orkney resident, recalls seeing the 'Merry Dancers', as they are known locally, over Scapa Flow early that night: 'I was out walking with a cousin and we recited Aytoun's lines:

Fearful lights that never beckon,
Save when kings and heroes die.

opposite phenomenon occurred when the tide was rising. Slack water, when the current was about to reverse itself, began 25 minutes before high and low water.

On the night of October 13, 1939, high water in Kirk Sound was at 2333.* Conditions for penetrating the anchorage would therefore be ideal shortly after 2300 hours. *U-47* came ghosting in towards Rose Ness right on time. But Lt. Prien did not have the Pentland Firth to himself. Out of the night loomed a ship, forcing *U-47* to dive to avoid possible detection. Lt. Prien later noted in his log that he could not make out the ship in either of his periscopes, despite the brightness of the night and the fact that she carried navigation lights.†

The difference between the success and failure of an undertaking often depends on factors which nobody could expect to foresee or cater for. The encounter with the mystery ship off Rose Ness caused a delay of half an hour and meant the passage through Kirk Sound would now have to be made with a following tide, a daunting prospect given a submarine's habit of yawing about under these conditions.

On the other hand, but for the delay *U-47*'s mission would almost certainly have ended in the disaster foreseen at U-boat HQ. For, at the time Lt. Prien was forced to submerge with the narrows of Kirk Sound three miles away, Chief Warden Alfred Flett of the Civil Defence was walking along the normally deserted north shore of the Sound, returning to his home in St Mary's after a special mission.

Earlier the last ship movement of the day had taken place at

* The time of high water was 2338 according to the *Royal Oak* Board of Inquiry. The above corrected time was supplied by Commander Nisbet Glen, RN, superintendent of the Tidal Branch of the Ministry of Defence Hydrographic Department.

† Trotz der sehr hellen Nacht und der brennenden Lichter kann ich den Dampfer in keinem der beiden Seerohre ausmachen.' The ship was almost certainly one of the neutral vessels which made regular use of the Pentland Firth for passages between the North Sea and Atlantic.

2024 with the sailing of the cruiser *Calypso*, and some time after that – he is not sure precisely when – the telephone rang in Warden Flett's home. It was ARP headquarters at Kirkwall with an order which was urgent, even if 40 years later it also sounds somewhat quaint. 'We've had a report that German aircraft are dropping mines in the eastern approaches to Scapa Flow,' he was told. 'Take a walk out towards the open sea and let us know if you can hear anything.'

Warden Flett welcomed the instruction as a break from his routine task of ensuring that the blackout was correctly observed in St Mary's. To be fair, he found the local residents co-operative, but the same could not be said, in Warden Flett's view, of O Company of the 7th (Mar and Mearns) Battalion of the Gordon Highlanders.

O Company, consisting largely of untrained men, had descended on St Mary's at the very start of the war. They lived in tents behind the Drill Hall, they used the kitchen of the Drill Hall as a guardroom, and they were responsible for guarding 'vulnerable points', which, generally speaking, meant points at which telephone cables disappeared under the sea to emerge in some other part of the Orkneys.

One of these points was at Howequoy Head where Kirk Sound broadens out into Scapa Flow. Warden Flett had discovered the Gordons with lights on in their tents at Howequoy. His protests about this and other incidents had not, he felt, been treated with the seriousness they deserved. Basically, it seemed to Warden Flett that we would have a better chance of winning the war if O Company went over to the enemy. When the occasion demanded, they were inclined to say: 'Come oot and see if Ah ken ye', rather than using the more military: 'Advance friend and be recognised'; they had shot a local cat in mistake for a German commando; and they had arrested Warden Flett himself in mistake for a German spy. The arrest had happened on just such a night as this when Warden Flett was out on a similar mission. A sergeant and two privates had taken him into custody, marched him to the Drill Hall and kept him under guard for an hour until their C.O., Captain Innes Stuart, appeared from his billet at the other end of the village and said he could be released.

On the night of October 13, 1939, Warden Flett strolled out to the seaward end of Kirk Sound, listened, heard nothing and strolled home again. At the Drill Hall, the dance was well under way. 'I don't remember any Northern Lights,' says Mr Flett, 'but it was a very clear night, considering there was no moon, and there was a very high tide. It was just about full when I got back to St Mary's.'

The height of the tide and the clearness of the night made him think about U-boats. Although the Admiralty took a more optimistic view, nobody in St Mary's had any doubts about the vulnerability of Kirk Sound: apart from local vessels, German trawlers had used it regularly to enter and leave Scapa Flow between the wars. It was right on the stroke of 2330 when Warden Flett reached home. He says: 'I remember quite distinctly remarking to my wife: "If ever there was a night for a submarine to come up, this is it."'

One minute later, *U-47* re-surfaced off Rose Ness.

Robbie Tullock had been right in thinking that he faced a long day. It was getting on for midnight before he finished the last scheduled trip in his taxi and made for home. On the way he was waved down by two young men who worked at the Royal Hotel and recognised his car.

'There's a dance at St Mary's,' they said. 'Will you take us down?'

Mr Tullock refused: with another job at six o'clock in the morning, he was anxious to get to bed.

'Aw, come on,' they pleaded. 'We've been working all day and we're fed up. We want a bit of fun.'

Mr Tullock still refused, but they argued some more and eventually he changed his mind and said: 'All right, jump in.'

It is arguable that, if he had stuck to his original decision, the whole story of that night might have worked out very differently and the controversy which has surrounded the loss of *Royal Oak* for 40 years would not have existed. Mr Tullock drove first to the Royal Hotel, where he picked up a couple of girls on the staff who also wanted to go to the dance, then he took the road south, past the RDF station at Netherbutton and on down to the shores of Kirk Sound. At that time, he says, the night was so bright – 'All the hills and fields were lit up' – that he was surprised when I told him there had been no moon.

Inside Scapa Flow were 51 vessels of the Royal Navy, 18 of which might be described as fighting ships – *Royal Oak*, the heavy cruiser *Belfast*, the light cruisers *Aurora, Cardiff, Caledon, Colombo* and *Delhi*, the Tribal class destroyers *Somali, Ashanti, Mashona, Eskimo* and *Tartar* (which had defects), the minesweepers *Hazard, Hebe, Seagull, Sharpshooter* and *Speedy*, and the A/A ship *Curlew*. With the exception of those on watch, nearly all of their crews had turned in for the night. They slept soundly. Apart from the danger of air attack, they knew they were safe in Scapa Flow.

On the night of October 13–14, 1939, there were, in fact, no fewer than 11 flaws in the Scapa Flow defences (see Appendix B) which might have been exploited by a U-boat to gain access to the anchorage – through, under and around booms and via the eastern entrances where there were no minefields, coast watchers, guns, searchlights or patrol vessels.

Kirk Sound, which had been selected for *U-47*'s attempt, was supposedly sealed by three wrecks. Taking them from south to north, there was the *Minich*, which had been broken up by the tides; the *Thames* (bows pointing south); and the *Soriano* (bows pointing north). From the bows of *Soriano* stretched a metal hawser attached to her anchor, which had been placed close to the north shore. Between the stern of *Thames* and the stern of *Soriano* there was a gap 136 feet wide. This had been sealed off a month earlier by linking the sterns of the two ships with a 12-inch hemp and an arrangement of heavy wires dangling at various depths. In addition, two more wires ran diagonally across the gap from the sterns of the two ships and were attached to massive anchors on the seabed.

These arrangements, however, still left Kirk Sound highly vulnerable. On the night of October 13–14, with its exceptionally high tide, there was still a gap 200 feet wide, offering a depth of 24 feet at high water, north of *Soriano*, and another gap, 400 feet wide, to the south of *Thames*. A U-boat using this second gap could count on a depth of 33–35 feet at *low* water *(U-47* drew 15½ feet).

Both Admiral Forbes, C.-in-C., Home Fleet, and Admiral French, ACOS, had shown active concern about the situation. Back in the summer, Admiral Forbes had sent a submission of protest to the Admiralty following a decision not to spend any more money on blockships. He complained that 'three large-scale surveys of Kirk and Skerry Sounds show that three straight channels exist through which enemy submarines or destroyers could enter Scapa Flow and attack the Fleet.' Admiral Forbes went on to quote from a letter which Admiral French, then ACOS delegate, had written to him following a recent visit of inspection to Scapa Flow; It said: '. . . I went down to Kirk and Skerry Sounds and went in and out of both of them on a young west-going tide in a picket boat. I would have no hesitation in doing either of them in a submarine or destroyer provided I could see and select slack water to do it in. Under these conditions it's complete rot talking about the swirls and eddies putting you on the beach or sunken ships. The sunken ships provide you with an excellent beacon.'

This submission caused the Admiralty to modify its views. Two more blockships were ordered, the *Cape Ortegal* and the *Lake Neuchatel*. On October 13, *Cape Ortegal* was already in position in Skerry Sound: *Lake Neuchatel*, destined to seal off the 400-ft southern gap which Lt. Prien would use for his escape, was scheduled to arrive that very weekend and be placed in position a few days later.

The rest of the Scapa Flow defences were in a similar state of disarray. To guard the Royal Navy's main base, Admiral French had a patrol force consisting of six Fleet drifters, two of which were usually boiler-cleaning at any given time. On the night of October 13–14, only two of the six drifters were in use. One was patrolling at Hoxa, one of the two southern entrances to the Flow. The Hoxa entrance, a mile and a half wide, was vulnerable in three ways to penetration by a U-boat. At the western end of the boom was a wide gap with 15 feet or more of water at high water; the boom itself did not reach the sea bed (it was 35 feet above the sea bed at high water springs); and no hydrophone or Asdic watch was kept when the boom was open. The other drifter was at the Hoy entrance, 1.7 miles wide, the north-west entrance to the Flow. Here, as well as a boom, there was a gap 500 feet wide, offering 30 feet of water, at the southern end of the boom. Neither at Hoxa nor at Hoy was a watch kept from the shore.

One can only feel sympathy for Admiral French. He did not have sufficient patrol vessels; he had no anti-submarine officer; his Chief of Staff did not arrive until October 13, just a few hours before *Royal Oak* was sunk; he was overwhelmed with administrative work and most of his officers had emerged from retirement and, in many cases, very long retirement. The situation is still a vivid memory for Commander Charles Harper, RN, who was the Admiral's assistant secretary at the time. 'One of the officers on the Admiral's staff had only one arm, having lost the other in the first World War, and another did not even have a uniform,' he told me. 'As *Iron Duke*'s ensign was lowered at sunset, he used to salute by raising his bowler hat. He was still wearing his bowler when he went over the side on October 17 after *Iron Duke* was bombed and holed and had to be beached.'

The unwillingness of the government to spend money on

defence, allied to various changes of plan and an unrealistic assessment of the range of German bombers, had helped to ensure that the land defences of Scapa Flow, under the nominal control of the Army, were as frail as the Navy's. On the night of October 13–14, they consisted of a laughable total of 16 guns, none of which could be fired without the permission of ACOS, and five coastal defence searchlights, all of which pointed out to sea and could not be elevated. The Army had only recently been given permission to switch the searchlights on from time to time, without asking ACOS, in order to make certain that the Orkneys were not about to be invaded.

In 1937 it had been agreed that, in the event of war, Rosyth was to be the main base of the Home Fleet with three battlecruisers and three aircraft carriers stationed at Scapa Flow. A year later, however, it was decided to leave the final choice to the C.-in-C., Home Fleet. He settled for Scapa Flow. It was generally accepted that, should there be air attacks, the Fleet would defend itself with its own guns. Even as late as August, 1939, it was believed that Scapa Flow was at the maximum range for German bombers and the anchorage was unlikely to be raided or, if it were, the raids would be minor ones. By September 3, this view had changed dramatically and the Chiefs of Staff agreed in principle that 80 heavy AA guns, 53 light AA guns, 108 searchlights and as many AA balloons as were required should be provided for the defence of Scapa Flow. The first guns under this programme were due to be loaded at Portsmouth on October 18 and the first searchlights at Aberdeen on October 22.

Thus, on the night of October 13–14, there were eight 4.5-inch AA guns on Hoy to defend the oil fuel depot; two 6-inch guns and one 4.7-inch gun, plus three searchlights, at Stanger Head at the entrance to Hoxa Sound; two 6-inch guns and two searchlights at Ness in the north-east corner of the Flow; and three 40-mm Bofors guns at Netherbutton to defend the RDF station. The searchlights were set in emplacements of corrugated iron and the war diary of the Orkney (Fortress)

Company, RE (TA), which was responsible for manning them, recorded rather plaintively that the shutters of the emplacements were so heavy that, in a gale, a Searchlight Operator 'unassisted may be unable to open them'. When this company was made responsible for manning rifle positions at Stanger Head in the event of a German landing, the war diary complained: 'The problem of effective defence – did the need arise – would have been aggravated by the fact that the allowance of small arms ammunition was only five rounds per man.'

Living conditions were terrible. The officer commanding one battery of four AA guns to the west of Lyness naval base was Captain Pat Scott, OBE, TD, DL, now managing director of the Highland Park Distillery at Kirkwall. 'We lived and slept in tents dating from 1915,' he recalls. Shortly before the outbreak of war, the 5th/7th Battalion, the Gordon Highlanders, had been divided, with most of the trained troops going to the 5th Battalion. Four officers and 155 other ranks, mostly raw recruits, from the 7th Battalion arrived in the Orkneys on September 7. Among the members of O Company, stationed at St Mary's, was Private William Anderson of Glenanan, Aberdeenshire. 'Our first meal when we arrived was tinned herring, and the smell in our mess tins lasted for days,' he remembers. 'We seemed to get a lot of tinned herring in our rations, but the country grocers' vanmen were quite willing to swop them for something else and some of the lads weren't slow at going and pinching a hen.

'I remember a few of us trying to wash with face towels and cold water under the village pump in St Mary's and we didn't get a bath for weeks. Eventually it was arranged for us to have baths at the Highland Park Distillery. One of the big tubs that was normally used for making whisky was filled with hot water and we jumped in, ten at a time.'

Lieut.-Colonel (then Major) D. Polson Hall, second-in-command of the 7th Battalion, was at Aberdeen when the Orkney detachment assembled to board a ship for Kirkwall and immediately christened them the 'Odds and Sods'. Later in the month he was sent up to the Orkneys to see how the 'Odds and Sods' were settling in. On his return he reported that he considered the situation a 'shambles'. 'They were doing their best, considering that the officers and NCOs were inexperienced and the troops, to a very large extent, recruits and untrained,' he told me. 'But they hadn't been issued with any ordnance stores for cooking and protection against the elements, and there weren't enough trained cooks to go around all the vulnerable points that had to be guarded.' Among the vulnerable points were selected telephone poles. He also reported that he considered 'guarding a telephone pole a complete waste of time when there were miles of unguarded overhead lines'.

That was Scapa Flow on the night of October 13–14, 1939, the Scapa Flow which Admiral Dönitz believed to be so well protected that 'the Admiralty, with all its great experience in these matters, and the Commander-in-Chief of the Home Fleet, must have complete confidence in the effectiveness of the measures taken and felt quite sure that the British warships were perfectly secure in their anchorage'.

U-47 was having a rough passage in the following tide, despite being trimmed down to reduce her buoyancy. Lt. Prien had decided to make his penetration by the gap to the north of the blockships and, way behind schedule, now found himself being borne along at 'unbelievable speed' by a current that flowed faster by the minute. It foamed against the wire which stretched from the bow of *Soriano* to her anchor close to the shore. At the moment Lt. Prien spotted the obstruction, *U-47* yawed towards the shore and grounded while the current rammed her stern hard against the anchor cable. Lt. Prien blew his ballast and diving tanks.* *U-47* hung for a moment. Then, with rudder hard to port and the cable holding her stern, her bow came back on course and her stern scraped free. The defences of Kirk Sound had been breached.

---

* This incident does not appear in most accounts of Lt. Prien's mission, but his log says: 'Die vorgefluteten Tauchbunker und Zellen werden ausgeblasen.'

Around the corner at the far end of the village appeared the lights of Robbie Tullock's taxi . . .

It is 200 yards to St Mary's general store and post office from the point at which the Kirkwall road joins the shore. Robbie Tullock covered the ground in a matter of seconds, turned left into Hall Road beside the post office and drove up the 70-yard slight incline to the Drill Hall, where he dropped his passengers off. From inside the hall came the sound of music. At the door stood three guards, members of O Company, wearing greatcoats and tam o'shanters and carrying rifles with fixed bayonets. They were chatting to some girls and readjusting the blackout curtain whenever anyone went in and out of the hall. It struck Robbie Tullock as a peculiar place for armed guards to be.*

Once he had been paid, he drove forwards and backwards a couple of times to turn around. At the bottom of Hall Road, he stopped before turning right into the shore road, and remained there for an appreciable time, his one masked headlamp shining on the water. 'I had never seen such a high tide there before,' he told me when I finally found him. 'I looked out across Kirk Sound. The visibility was good – it was still a very bright night – but I didn't see anything. There had been some talk about whether it might be possible for a U-boat to get into the Flow, but it had not occurred to me that a submarine might enter on the surface. I assumed if there was an attempt the U-boat would be submerged.

'I didn't get out of the car and, after a while, it struck me that such a bright night would be a good one for an air attack on the

---

* It is not clear whether the guards had just come off duty or had perhaps wandered round from the kitchen at the rear of the hall, which they used as a guardroom. When Mr Tullock heard next morning of the loss of *Royal Oak*, he thought – wrongly – that the guards might have been responsible for keeping a lookout at Kirk Sound and, if he came forward, was questioned and revealed what the guards had been doing, they might be court-martialled and shot. That is why he kept silent for nearly 40 years.

RDF station at Netherbutton, which was between me and home. I switched off my headlamp because I could see quite well without it and drove off at full speed, using just my sidelights. But, after I had passed the RDF station, it grew dark and began to rain. I remember quite clearly switching on my headlight again and the windscreen wipers. It was about twenty to one when I got back to Kirkwall.'

Out in Kirk Sound, *U-47*, using only her electric motors, slid quietly past St Mary's and rounded Skaildaquoy Point.* The time was 0027. It was Lt. Prien's custom always to keep his crew informed about what was happening. Now he announced briefly: 'We are in.' Laid out before him was the vast, historic anchorage of Scapa Flow – and there wasn't a ship in sight.

* One wild December night I went out to Burray on the seaward side of Kirk Sound to talk to a man who claims to have actually seen *U-47* making her entrance. Jock Park says that, on the night in question, he and his brother Ronnie had rowed down to Skerry Sound, adjoining Kirk Sound, to indulge in the honoured Orkney pursuit known as 'wreckin'' – the removal of anything of value – aboard the blockship *Cape Ortegal*. His story is: 'About midnight, I looked across towards St Mary's and saw what I thought was a tug passing through Kirk Sound. She was very low in the water. Next morning, when I heard about *Royal Oak*, I realised that what I thought was a tug must have been a submarine.' I have not included this incident in the main narrative because Mr Park's insistence that it was low water at the time must inevitably create some doubt about whether his recollection is accurate. I think he is probably right about the U-boat, wrong about the low water, but it is not easy to argue tides with an Orkney fisherman.

4

What the Hell was that, then?

There are three basic aspects to the events which occurred in Scapa Flow in the next hundred minutes or so: the recollection of the *Royal Oak* survivors . . . the German story . . . and the facts, many of which are printed here for the first time.

It would be naive to expect all three aspects to tally. The impressions of men who have had a 29,000-ton battleship sink under them in less than a quarter of an hour must inevitably be coloured by the experience. Nor can one expect Lt. Prien and his crew, cruising around the main anchorage of the Home Fleet in the middle of the night and expecting that death or capture might be their imminent reward, to be the most reliable of witnesses. The passage of 40 years has not helped either.

Not long ago Herbert Herrmann paid his first visit to the Orkneys since 1939, went down to Kirk Sound, and later told me that it gave him 'the creeps' just to look at it. 'I don't know if you can put yourself in our position,' he explained. 'If you were breaking into somebody's house, you wouldn't be yourself. You'd see things that weren't there, you'd hear things that weren't there, the slightest noise would make you jump. That was how we felt. This was my first trip, but everybody thought much the same as I did: "Bloody hell, we'll never get out again. This is the end." We knew two U-boats which had attempted the same feat in the first World War had been destroyed. That sticks in your mind. You were afraid, you were always afraid, and wondered if each trip would be your last.'

The following account of events in Scapa Flow is based upon Lt. Prien's log. The criticisms of the *Royal Oak* survivors, plus the facts, have been interpolated without, at this stage, any real attempt to resolve the discrepancies which arise.

When *U-47* cleared Howequoy Head and entered Scapa Flow, the nearest ship to the U-boat was *Royal Oak*, anchored some 5,600 yards away, west of north, with her entire silhouette (bow to north-east wind) visible from the U-boat's bridge. Yet there has never been any suggestion that Lt. Prien or his crew saw the battleship at this point, The obvious deduction must therefore be that visibility was less than 5,600 yards.

U-47 headed westwards towards the main Fleet anchorage on the far side of the Flow, bounded to the south by the island of Flotta, to the west by the island of Fara, and to the north-west by the island of Cava. But, after approximately three miles, Lt. Prien decided to abandon his approach, a course of action to which he devotes some space in his log. The entry reads:

> *It is disgustingly bright. The whole bay is fabulous to survey. To the south of Cava lies nothing. I go farther in. To port I recognise the Hoxa Sound guard, to which the boat must very soon offer itself as a target. Then everything would be lost; at present south of Cava no ships can be made out, although everything is clearly recognisable at a great distance. 0055* So, decision: South of Cava lies nothing, therefore, before any prospect of success is placed at risk, achievable results must be obtained.†*

* This time, and the time of the two subsequent attacks on *Royal Oak*, have been queried in pencil after the log was typed, presumably because they do not tie in with the distances covered by *U-47* according to the map which accompanies the log.

† 'Es ist widerlich hell. Die ganze Bucht ist fabelhaft zu übersehen. Südlich Cava liegt nichts. Ich laufe noch näher. Da erkenne ich an B.B. die Hoxa-Sound Bewachung, für die das Boot als Zielscheibe in den nächsten Sekunden erscheinen muss. Damit wäre alles umsonst, zumal sich südlich Cava noch immer keine Schiffe ausmachen lassen, obwohl sonst auf weiteste Entfernungen alles klar erkennbar ist. 0055. Also Entschluss: Südlich Cava liegt nichts, deshalb, bevor jede Aussicht auf Erfolg aufs Spiel gesetzt wird, müssen erreichbare Erfolge durchgeführt werden.'

It is this early in the proceedings that the *Royal Oak* survivors part company with Lt. Prien. They say it was not a spectacularly bright night, with visibility in excess of five miles, but a dark night – and, on the evidence available, it is difficult not to agree with them.

The only other person to suggest that the night was bright rather than just clear is Robbie Tullock, and even he says that it had grown dark and begun to rain by the time he returned to his home in Kirkwall at about 0040 hours. Marine Alan Lawrence, who stayed talking with a friend on the deck of *Royal Oak* until around midnight, remembers the night as dark. 'I could just make out the shore about half a mile away, but only because the cliffs were even darker than the sky,' he says.

This assessment is supported, at least by implication, by the silent testimony of the logs of most of the naval vessels in Scapa Flow at the time. When the weather was noted as a matter of routine with the change of watch at midnight, nobody thought the visibility worthy of special mention, although watchkeepers in harbour tend to seize on anything to break the monotony, and the estimate of cloud cover ranged from 25–75 per cent to more than 75 per cent.

But Lt. Prien's assertion that he could be absolutely certain at a range of five miles that there were no ships south of Cava raises more serious difficulties than this. Firstly, the nearest and quite the largest ship to him was still *Royal Oak*, now some 6,500 yards to the north-east. Yet there has again never been any suggestion that the crew of *U-47* could see the battleship at this range. And secondly, despite Lt. Prien's confident statement to the contrary, there *were* ships south of Cava.

Admittedly, they would have been difficult to detect, bow-on to a north-east wind against a background of land, but when Lt. Prien abandoned his approach to the main Fleet anchorage he was 6,600 yards and 7,500 yards respectively from the cruisers

Caledon and *Belfast*, anchored about a thousand yards off the north shore of Flotta; and roughly 9,200 yards from *Delhi* and *Colombo*, anchored close to each other between south and south-east of Cava.*

In the light of these facts it seems fair to conclude that Lt. Prien's estimate of visibility was at the very least exaggerated.

U-47 made a turn to port and retraced her course towards Kirk Sound. Apart from the throb of the U-boat's engines, the Flow remained silent. Lt. Prien cut diagonally across the face of the Sound, then turned north by the coast. At this point, *U-47* was just over 5,000 yards from *Royal Oak*. For yet a third time, there is no suggestion, and never has been, that the battleship was visible at this range.

The only other naval vessel in the north-east corner of the Flow at the time was the comparatively tiny, 25-year-old sea-plane carrier *Pegasus*, anchored 1,500 yards virtually due north of *Royal Oak*. This is the position given by the bearings in her log: 205°, 9.2 cables (1,840 yards) from Scapa Pier light. But, according to Lt. Prien, gradually a shadow, followed by a shape – then two shapes – came into view.

Two battleships are lying there, further inshore destroyers at anchor. Cruisers not to be seen, attack on the two fat fellows. Distance 3,000 metres [note: roughly 3280 yards]. Estimated depth, 7.5 metres.

---

* The anchor bearings given in the cruisers' logs are: *Belfast*, Fara 285°, Diamond Beacon 125½°, A buoy 244°; *Caledon*, Calf of Flotta 085°, Beacon 165°; *Colombo*, Fara Church 003°, South House Cava 331°, Barrel of Butter 024°; and *Delhi*, E. Point Cava 354°, N. Point Fara 262°, N. Point Risa 293°. The position of the Diamond Beacon can be confirmed with the postal authorities at Kirkwall and the stump of wood to which it was attached is still visible on Flotta. *Cardiff*, whose anchor bearings are missing from her log, was probably somewhere close to *Delhi* and *Colombo*. Vice-Admiral Sir Ian Hogg, KCB, DSC, RN (retd.), who was serving in the cruiser at the time, thinks she must have been anchored 'well over to the west of the Flow as we had no sight or sound' of the sinking *of Royal Oak*.

Impact firing. 0116 [time queried in pencil, 0058 suggested, names of Repulse and Royal Oak added in pencil.] One shot at the northern ship, two at the southern. After a good 3½ minutes, a torpedo detonates on the northern ship; of the other two nothing is to be seen. About 0121 [time queried in pencil, 0102 suggested]. Shot from the stern tube. *

Again, there are a number of factual errors in this entry, which is not, of course, to say that the errors were not made in good faith, particularly if it was not a spectacularly bright night. There were no destroyers anchored closer inshore: all of the destroyers were anchored in Gutter Sound, all of the minesweepers in Long Hope, nearly 10 miles away on the other side of the Flow. Nor was there a northern 'fat fellow', anchored, according to the *U-47* map, some 600 yards beyond *Royal Oak*.

None of the *Royal Oak* survivors attempted to reach any inshore destroyers or the northern 'fat fellow' anchored close to them. The inshore destroyers and the northern 'fat fellow' did not send boats to *Royal Oak*. Nor did the northern 'fat fellow' have to undergo repairs as a result of this attack.

The whereabouts of ships under repair during the war was concealed by giving them job numbers, which were announced in the weekly *Confidential Admiralty Fleet Orders*. The only 'fat fellow' mentioned in the weeks immediately after the loss *of Royal Oak* was *Hood*, allocated the number D57 at the end of October. The battlecruiser subsequently spent from November 11 to November 28,

---

* 'Dort liegen zwei Schlachtschiffe, weiter unter Land Zerstörer vor Anker. Kreuzer nicht auszumachen, Angriff auf die beiden Dicken. Abstand 3,000m, Eingestellte Tiefe 7.5m. Aufschlagzündung. 0116 (?) 0058. Ein Schuss auf den nördlichen, zwei Schuss auf den südlich liegenden losgemacht. Es detoniert nach gut 3½ Minuten ein Torpedo auf dem nördlich liegenden Schlachtschiff, von den anderen beiden ist nichts zu sehen! Kehrt! 0121 (?) 0102. Heckschuss.'

1939, in Devonport Dockyard where, according to her *Ship's Book*, which lists all alterations and repairs, she was fitted with a new plotting table, had some work done to the Admiral's and Captain's sea cabins, and had extra weather protection fitted to the Admiral's bridge.

Lt. Prien's account of this first attack on *Royal Oak* does provide some additional, and fairly precise, information about visibility, if one assumes – which seems logical – that he would not in the dangerous circumstances approach any closer than necessary to his target.

At a range of 5,000 yards, he could not see *Royal Oak*. At a range of 3,280 yards (estimated) he was able to carry out an attack on the battleship. In actual fact, the range was probably slightly greater than that. The speed of G7e torpedoes, the type used, was 30 knots, a thousand yards a minute. This suggests a range of just over 3,500 yards – which puts *U-47* 5,000 yards from *Pegasus*. The implication must therefore be that the British version of events (Lt. Prien mistook *Pegasus* for *Repulse*) is more generous than realistic. If Lt. Prien and his crew could not see *Royal Oak* (620 feet long, 29,150 tons) from a range of 5,000 yards when they began to proceed north by the coast, how could they see the much smaller *Pegasus* (360 feet long, 6,900 tons) from a similar range a few minutes later?*

Lt. Prien was right in thinking that the only one of the torpedoes fired in his first attack which reached a target struck the bow of a ship. It did not strike the bow of *Repulse*, which was not there; it did not strike the bow of *Pegasus*, which he could not see; it blew a hole 40 to 50 feet wide and three plates deep in

* The torpedo was G7e torpedo no. 2874, manufactured by the Berliner Maschinenbau Aktiengesellschaft, previously known as L. Schwarzkopf. The electric motor, gears and double-bladed propeller, still joined together and recovered from alongside the wreck of *Royal Oak*, have been identified by experts as part of a German electrical torpedo of pre-war manufacture.

the starboard bow of *Royal Oak*, starting one plate below the waterline.

The explosion came at 0104 and was followed immediately by a deafening rumble as both anchor chains ran out. Leading Signalman Fossey, on watch on the flag-deck, saw a spout of water shoot into the air and cascade onto the forecastle-deck. Below, opinions about the intensity and effect of the explostion varied from one part of the ship to another. Forward, men were blown out of their hammocks and a steel shelf snapped in two. Amidships, Petty Officer Dick Kerr recalls having the impression that it sounded like 'a large zinc bath falling on the deck of the Wardroom bathroom' above his head. In the stern, where most of the officers had turned in for the night, it felt as if a giant terrier had picked *Royal Oak* up in its teeth and shaken her.

Royal Oak's captain, Captain William Benn, went forward to investigate, and was informed that air gushing from the vents of the inflammable store suggested that there had been an internal explosion and the store was flooding. The matter was not at this time considered serious: the trim of the ship had not been affected and the flooding could easily be contained. While arrangements were made for dealing with the problem, the 'buzz' which swept the ship was that one of the CO_2 bottles in the refrigeration plant, also in the bows, had gone up. Many of the crew, reassured, simply turned in again: others, more cautiously minded and thinking that a German plane might have glided over and dropped a bomb, took refuge beneath the armoured deck, a decision which would shortly condemn them to death.

At the time of the first explosion, Chief ERA Charlie Cartwright was asleep in his hammock next to the anchor cable locker: 'The cable ran out with a great roar. I thought it was going to burst out of its locker. The whole place shook and there was dust everywhere. Then the noise stopped as suddenly as it had started. I couldn't figure out what was supposed to be going on, and in the end I gave up thinking about it, turned over and went back to sleep.'

Vincent Marchant, then 18, jumped out of his hammock in the seamen's mess, next to the boys' mess, amidships on the starboard side, and went forward in his vest and underpants to see what was happening. Outside the cells, from which two prisoners had been released as a precaution, there was smoke and 'a funny smell', but the Master-of-Arms was telling everyone in sight: 'Get back. There's no need to panic.'

George White, now security officer at the British Embassy in Amman, was asleep in the 6-inch gun casement immediately above the boys' messdeck. 'I was an Instructor Boy, exactly a month short of my 17th birthday,' he told me. 'The boys' messdeck was full to overflowing and I decided to sleep in the casemate because the air was fresher there. I think that is why I was one of 32 boys saved out of a total of 175. We all turned out after the first explosion but were ordered to turn in again a few minutes later by our PT instructor.'

Acting Petty Officer Tom Blundell had dozed off in a mood of quiet contentment. Apart from the war, it had been a good year for him: his first child had been born, a three-month-old daughter he had yet to see; he had been promoted; and, just a few hours earlier, he had picked up six and a half months' back promotion pay with the result that he had the astronomical sum of £13.1s. tucked away in his green money belt. His hammock was slung under a ladder with a large hatch above it and a manhole in the centre of the hatch. After the first explosion had woken him, he lay looking at the manhole for several minutes, wondering what might have happened. 'Then,' he says, 'I decided I had better turn out and go and see whether I was needed for a fire party.'

'Taffy' Davies, in the Marines' messdeck towards the stern, was worried: the explosion had seemed to him too violent not to be serious. 'I was in my hammock in a little passage which we used to call "The Junior NCO's Club" because about four corporals slung their hammocks in there. A corporal of the gangway I knew very well came along and I asked him: "What the hell was that, then?" "I dunno, Taff," he said. "There's a buzz that the CO_2 machine has gone up."

'Somehow I didn't like it. I got out of my hammock and dressed, even to putting my cap on. *Royal Oak* was a bastard of a ship: you weren't allowed on the upper deck, even in wartime, without your cap on. When I got just abaft of B turret I could hear a lot of noise on the fo'c'sle, clinking and the sound of hammers, and I thought I'd better not go blundering through because they'd only say: "Bloody Marines, in the way again." There was a screen door into the superstructure next to me. I was still a bit worried about going down below so I stepped inside the door and lit a cigarette. I couldn't see anyone on the fo'c'sle, just hear the noises, and the Flow itself was as black as a cow's gut.

'A stoker came up to me and said: "What the hell's going on, Royal?" I said: "I don't know, Stokes, haven't a clue. Someone told me the CO_2 machinery had gone up." "No fear, it hasn't," he said. "I've just come up from there."'

Down in the sick bay, SBA 'Lofty' Bendell was officially on duty, but, tired out like everyone else after the Fair Isle trip, had taken a chance and turned in. He was awakened shortly after the first explosion by someone asking for a cut on a leg to be attended to. 'How did you do that?' he asked. 'I was blown out of my hammock,' the man explained. 'Lofty' Bendell dressed the wound of his unexpected patient and told him to come back in the morning to see the Medical Officer. The man looked at him in disbelief. 'The bloody ship's sinking', he said. SBA Bendell said: 'Don't be wet', settled back into his cot and went to sleep again.

The explosion had been heard and felt aboard *Pegasus*, 1,500 yards away. Mechanician Rowley was one of the men it woke. 'It was as if we had been struck by a huge hammer,' he recalls.

'Some of my messmates and I jumped out of our hammocks, hastily slipped on anything handy and went on deck. It was dark, but we could just see the outline of *Royal Oak.*' John Laughton also heard the bang on shore. He was reading in bed at his home, Foveran, on the cliffs to the north *of Pegasus* and to the west of Scapa Pier. 'I got up and went outside to try to see what was happening,' he says. He was approximately 1,600 yards from *Pegasus*, 3,000 yards from *Royal Oak.* 'I could just make out the seaplane carrier, but I couldn't see *Royal Oak* at all,' he told me.*

Aboard the battleship, nearly 12 minutes had passed since the first explosion. A light was switched on to examine some baulks of timber floating in the sea near the starboard bow. 'Taffy' Davies finished his cigarette, flipped the butt over the side and thought to himself: 'Well, I can't think of any more excuses for stopping up here.' He still didn't feel very happy.

The torpedo fired from the stern tube of *U-47* also disappeared without trace. This was not an uncommon happening. At the start of the war, and for a considerable time afterwards, trackless German electrical torpedoes were extremely inefficient and prone to run too deep, run wild, explode prematurely or not explode at all. On October 30, 1939, for example, the commander of *U-56* fired a salvo of three at the battleship *Nelson*, and the distressing consequences are recorded by Admiral Dönitz in his memoirs: 'The crew of *U-56*, which, of course, was submerged at the time, clearly heard the noise of impact as the three torpedoes struck the *Nelson*. They all three failed to explode. The commander, who had delivered his attack with great daring when surrounded by 12 escorting destroyers, was

---

* Visibility would have been better looking up from the bridge of *U-47* than looking down into the Flow from a clifftop, and Mr Laughton's range of vision would, of course, have been reduced by the fact that his eyes were not yet accustomed to the darkness.

so depressed by this failure, in which he was no way to blame, that I felt compelled to withdraw him for the time being from active operations and employ him as an instructor at home.'

Lt. Prien, too, later claimed to have fired no fewer than eight torpedoes at a long line of overlapping transports in a Norwegian fiord on the night of April 15, 1940, without result. At about this time he also reported: 'Sighted *Warspite* and two destroyers and attacked the battleship with two torpedoes at a range of 900 yards. No success. As a result of the explosion of one of them at the end of its run, I was placed in a most awkward predicament and was pursued by destroyers coming from all directions.' On his return from this patrol, Lt. Prien protested that he could hardly be expected to 'fight with a dummy rifle'.

In Scapa Flow, *U-47*, with one torpedo still in the bow tubes, headed once again for Kirk Sound while two more torpedoes were loaded. By this time, Lt. Prien had been cruising around Scapa Flow for three quarters of an hour, he had torpedoed a battleship, yet there was still no sign of reaction in the anchorage. Off Howequoy Head, with everything still quiet, *U-47* turned to starboard and made her way north again for a second attack. On this occasion, the running time given for the torpedoes indicates that *U-47* went in closer, to 3,000 yards:

> . . . *three torpedoes from the bow. After three tense minutes comes the detonation on the nearer ship. There is a loud explosion, roar and rumbling. Then come columns of water, columns of fire, fragments fly through the air.* *

The butt of 'Taffy' Davies's cigarette had just fizzled out in the dark waters of Scapa Flow. He turned to go below. At that moment, *Royal Oak* shuddered under the impact of three

---

* '3 Bugschüsse. Nach je knappen 3 Minuten nach den Abschüssen die Detonationen auf dem näherliegenden Schiff. Da rollt, knallt, bumst and grummelt es gewaltig. Zunächts Wassersäulen, dann Feuersäulen, Broken fliegen durch die Luft.'

violent explosions. 'I think there was one, then a short space of seconds and two almost simultaneously,' he recalls. 'The old gal heeled over. She went over to port, then back to starboard, and almost at once there was a 20-degree slope on the deck.' The time was 0116. Anyone who hoped to save his life had 13 minutes to escape.

5

Daisy, Daisy

John Gatt, skipper of the civilian drifter *Daisy II*, moored on the port side of *Royal Oak*, had been awakened by the first explosion and came on deck. He called up to one of the watch: 'What happened?' Nobody could tell him. He went below, put on some clothes. When he came on deck again, somebody shouted down from *Royal Oak:* 'Raise steam immediately.' Skipper Gatt passed the order on to his engineer, one of his crew of five, and went forward. 'The first thing I noticed was pieces of wood floating past,' he recalled later. 'One of the watch asked what it was. I said it might be floating stuff from the beach as it was just after high water. The battleship put on a searchlight. A minute later there were three or four explosions on the starboard side, the flames went up to the height of her mast and she gave a terrible lurch at the same time . . .'

The first of the three explosions, roughly amidships on the starboard side, wiped out many of the boys in their messdeck above. The second, slightly further aft on the same side of the ship, caused most havoc in the stokers' messdeck: it blew a hole in the armoured deck and cut many men down where they stood, having just leaped from their hammocks. Others were severely burned. The third explosion, slightly further aft again, created similar destruction in the Marines' messdeck.

The electricity supply failed, plunging *Royal Oak* into darkness and making it impossible either to issue orders or send a signal for help. Cordite in one of the magazines ignited and a bright orange flame swept through the ship, cremating men who stood in its path and setting fire to hammocks, clothing, tables, curtains, anything that would burn.

For the comfort of the crew while in harbour, the normal glass scuttles in the portholes had been replaced with ventilators, held in position by two butterfly nuts, which allowed fresh air to enter but prevented any light from escaping. *Royal Oak* began to heel more rapidly as the sea cascaded in through the lowest ventilators, only 10 feet above the waterline. Within a minute or two of the three explosions on the far side of the ship from him, Skipper Gatt ordered *Daisy* to be cut adrift. When the warps were severed, however, she refused to budge: she was hard on the battleship's anti-torpedo blister and being lifted bodily out of the sea as *Royal Oak* rolled to starboard.

Down below, all was chaos as men blundered about in the darkness, seeking a means of escape. Some found a way out with ridiculous ease, some after a hard struggle. Others, when hope seemed gone, discovered themselves, as if by a miracle, before an exit that led to the open air and a chance, at least, to fight for their lives in the cold sea. A few escaped through portholes after unscrewing the butterfly nuts of the ventilators. By then *Royal Oak* had heeled over so far that they were able to walk quite easily across the near-horizontal port side of the ship and drop into the water.

Charlie Cartwright, in his hammock up towards the bow, remembers the series of three explosions, the lights going out, the ship heeling over rapidly, but most of the other details of that traumatic night have been obliterated by a combination of shock and the passing years. 'I know I found myself standing under an open hatch,' he told me. 'I could see stars. I went up the ladder and over the side into the sea.' That is virtually all he can recall.

In the seamen's mess, the three explosions started a stampede for the upper deck. 'It was like a charge of buffaloes,' Vincent Marchant remembers. 'By the time we reached the deck the ship had started to heel. I went straight across to the boom on the starboard side where there was a big launch tied up. I jumped in. The ship kept rolling over towards us and the bow rope of the launch went bar-taut. Someone shouted: "Cut us adrift", but nobody had a knife because we were all in our underpants. I could see the spotting top starting to hang over our heads so I decided the only thing to do was to dive into the sea and make a swim for it.'

George White retains the impression of 'huge fireballs' hurtling past the casemate after the second explosion: 'The lights went out and there was a lot of shouting in the darkness. I made for the ladder leading up to the galley flat and had just cleared the hatch when the third explosion occurred. A sheet of flame came through the hatch, striking the deckhead above. I can still remember the intense heat. All those on the ladders and climbing clear just fell back into the holocaust below them.' George White clambered out, hand-over-hand, onto the starboard boom and dropped into the launch, but he, too, decided it was safer in the water as the spotting top came over. 'I jumped into a sea of oil,' he told me, 'and started to strike out towards the shore. I could feel a slight suction from the ship taking water.'

Dick Kerr was knocked flat by the explosions and, when he picked himself to his feet, tried to escape with a number of men via the officers' bathroom and a door which led to the port battery. It wouldn't open: the heel of the ship had jammed the handles. Flames spread behind him, but, almost overcome by fumes, he kept wrestling with the door and kicking it. Finally, it burst open. Beyond lay another inferno. He charged straight into it, stumbled, almost fell, and came out the other side with half his hair missing and severe burns to his head, neck and hands although at the time he felt no pain. Outside, the deck was almost vertical, but he pulled himself up onto the port guardrail where he took off his jacket and trousers before walking across the side of the ship and plunging into the sea. His immediate aim was to put as much distance as possible between himself and *Royal Oak* in case he was sucked under when she went.

Tom Blundell had just started to dress when it seemed to him as if some immense force 'had lifted the whole ship and shaken her'. 'I had my jersey, socks and shoes on and was just reaching for my trousers,' he told me. 'There was a blast of air and a smell like explosives. The lights went out and I could hear men shouting. I did not feel any fear: I was just stupefied, shocked by the enormity of the explosions. By the time I came to my senses there was a queue of men struggling to get up the ladder and out through the manhole, one at a time.'

The hatch at the top of the ladder was sealed off by a steel plate when *Royal Oak* was in action. The toggle which held the plate open had not been fastened properly and, as the ship heeled, it slid across, cutting off the escape route. Somebody shouted: 'Let's try the ports.' 'There was a rush for the ship-wrights' mess,' Tom Blundell went on. 'Whoever had put the ventilators in position had made a good job of it: I thought I'd never get the nuts undone. When I finally succeeded and pulled myself up into the open air, the side of the ship was horizontal. I started walking and then I tripped, fell and rolled into the sea. It was freezing cold.' As he struck out towards the cliffs, just visible because they were blacker than the dark sky, he thought of his wife and the baby daughter he had not yet seen.

'Lofty' Bendell had just dozed off again after attending to his unexpected patient when he was hurled out of his cot and lay unconscious on the deck of the sick bay for several minutes. When he came to again, the ship was listing so much that it was no longer possible to walk. He and a companion crawled along on all fours until they found a ladder leading to a hatch, but the hatch refused to open. They crawled on in darkness to the POs' mess, where they became separated.

Bendell found himself in the mess pantry, looking at an open porthole which others had already used to make their escape. He climbed into the sink and was trying to drag himself through the opening when *Royal Oak* gave a final lurch, turned turtle and sank. The sea gushed in through the porthole and open door of the pantry, and Bendell, who had gone tumbling backwards in a shower of crockery and kitchen equipment, floated to the surface with the deck now above his head. The water around him rose rapidly for a few seconds, then stopped, held back by a bubble of air. He could breathe but he was trapped with only one possible means of escape – the open porthole now several feet below him. He dived, failed to find it, fought his way back to the surface for another lungful of precious air, dived a second time, again without success. When he resurfaced, his head bumped the deck and there was no sign of the bubble of air. 'I've had it now,' he thought, opened his mouth and gulped down some water, anxious only to make death as swift and easy as possible.

Marine 'Gillie' Potter turned out after the first explosion, but, reassured by the rumour about the CO_2 bottle, climbed back into his hammock. He was balanced on the edge of it, tucking himself in, when he was blown out again, fell on a dynamo fan and was knocked semi-conscious. He staggered to his feet with blood running down his face, and an injured back, shoulder and neck. 'As I got up,' he says, 'I saw this orange flame, like a great blowlamp. I wasn't in its path, but everyone who was went down like ninepins, dead. In front of me seemed to be a mass of flame and behind me the hammock netting caught fire. Everyone was scrambling to get out. We went aft, with a couple of mates more or less dragging me, and found a door blocked by a dynamo which had fallen over, but we managed to wrench it open. We went through the officers' cabins and up a ladder onto the upper deck.

'She was tilted so far over you couldn't walk on the upper deck: you had to crawl on your hands and knees. On the starboard side she was gunwales under and the water was full of men. We walked down the ship's side. It was cold after coming up from the warm messdeck – I was only in my singlet –

and, as I was about to make a jump into the sea, I saw the port propeller under me. I threw myself sideways and skidded down the barnacles into the water. If you want to know what it's like not to sit down for several days, I can tell you.'

'Taffy' Davies, fortunate to find himself already on deck, was at first puzzled and could not make up his mind what to do. 'I just stood there for a while,' he explained. 'I was a bit of a health-and-strength merchant in those days and could swim fairly well, but the Flow looked dark and cold. My first impulse was to run, but my old Dad always told me: "If you're in a panic, stop and count." So I stopped and I heard someone on the fo'c'sle say: "Make your way aft to the *Daisy*", and I thought that sounded like a good idea.

'When I reached the quarter-deck, the old gal must have been 25 or 30 degrees over. Dozens of men were diving into the drink and swimming to the *Daisy*, which struck me as a silly thing to do when the *Daisy* was still tied up alongside. Thinking about the generous way a grateful government treats its war widows, I climbed over the port guardrail and walked down the ship's side to the blister. Along the top of the blister was a guttering which we used to call a stringer. That gave me a bit of a grip among the barnacles and seaweed and I took a flying jump into the drifter.'

As *Royal Oak* heeled farther over, her spotting top came adrift, hurtled down on the launch on the starboard side and sank it. At about the same time, the *Daisy* was thrown clear and sent crashing stern first into the sea. The impact started her leaking, but not too badly. Skipper Gatt backed off, began to blow a whistle to indicate his position, then lit two gas lamps. Men in the sea, who had been singing *South of the Border* and *Run, Rabbit, Run* to keep their spirits up, changed the tune to *Daisy, Daisy, Give Me Your Answer Do* when the lights came on.

Aboard the drifter, 'Taffy' Davies was feeling guilty. 'It seemed to me that the *Oak* was bound to go, but there were still people sitting on the side,' he explained. 'That was the old naval discipline: you didn't do anything off your own bat, and I remember the thought running through my mind: "If she doesn't go, they're going to ask: 'What the hell were you doing sitting in the *Daisy*?' One of the things I recall most vividly of all was an officer – a midshipman, I imagine, from the sound of his voice – calling out in the darkness: "Wait for the order to abandon ship." I think the silly bugger was still saying it when the *Oak* rolled over and sank. She went with a whoosh. You could hear the stuff breaking loose inside her and the 15-inch shells going boom-boom, boom, boom-boom.'

Apart from the *Daisy*, there were now only two vessels in the vicinity, *Royal Oak*'s picket boat and Rear-Admiral Henry Blagrove's gig, which, still with its cover on, had floated off the quarter-deck. With more than a hundred men on board, double the number it was designed to take, the picket boat turned turtle, trapping some of *Royal Oak*'s crew inside it. Those thrown into the water tried to clamber back onto the upturned hull, which eventually sank under their weight and was not seen again. A few made for the waterlogged gig, which kept turning over and over, but nobody occupied this precarious sanctuary for long: it was warmer in the sea than out of it.

One who came to that conclusion was Chief ERA Wilson. When all the lights went out on *Royal Oak*, he and about 40 other men had managed to find their way up a ladder with the aid of the torch which some vague feeling of unease had impelled him to buy in Kirkwall a few hours earlier. He first sought refuge in the picket boat, was thrown into the sea when it capsized, and, in the ensuing confusion, with men trying to grab each other for support, lost all his clothing except a waistbelt and one leg of his pyjamas. He managed to break free and, fearing he would be unwittingly drowned by his own shipmates, made for the gig. But, after climbing onto its keel, he decided he would freeze to death there, lowered himself back into the sea and clung on. Even then, he said later, he was so cold 'I could feel every bone of my body.' The *Daisy* eventually found him.

Of Skipper Gatt, 'Taffy' Davies says admiringly: 'He was as calm as if he was on a milk round, just giving a little touch of the engine every now and again and hauling anyone aboard who came paddling past. The injured and the ones who were coughing their guts up with fuel oil we put down in the fish hold. The deck also grew more and more crowded with people taking turns to get near the cowling and the warmth of the engine. Many were close to tears and asking: "Why doesn't somebody come and help us? They must know by now that the ship has gone." I was one of the most popular blokes because I still had my packet of Craven A in my pocket. In 1967, when we had our first reunion at Portsmouth, a fellow came up to me and said: "Do you know a corporal named Davies?" I said I did. He said: "I want to meet him. He saved my life. I was dying for a smoke and he was the only bloke with a packet of fags."'

In the meantime, Vincent Marchant, having dived over the side of the threatened launch, had decided to make for the cliffs which he could just make out, a dark shadow against the night sky a thousand yards away. 'The oil was like treacle and I was covered in it,' he says, 'but I kept plugging away. I had another bloke with me. I kept encouraging him, but halfway to the shore he disappeared. Once I was out of the water I scrambled up the cliff face. I suppose it was about 40 feet. Then about 50 yards inland, I came to a barbed wire fence, but I just didn't have the strength to climb it. I was knackered. I lay there I don't know how long before I heard a voice. Some cutters with signal lamps had appeared below the cliff. I shouted down to them and they shouted back: "Hang on, don't move." About half an hour later a stretcher party appeared with a bottle of brandy, gave me a tot and carried me off to the cottage hospital at Kirkwall. I was in there a week.'

George White, who had also struck out for the shore, had been swimming for 30 minutes or more when he bumped into a dead body, face down in the water. 'It was clad in a watch coat,' he told me. 'I can well remember hanging on to the short belt these coats have at the back. I don't know how long I stayed clutching the belt, but I'm sure the rest from swimming played a great part in saving my life. Next I heard cries for help and saw someone swimming towards me. I was scared of having anyone come too close. I pushed the body towards him and told him to hold on to it. Then I started swimming for the shore again. I could faintly make out the dark silhouette of the cliffs against the sky, and I tried to make for a beach where the boys on board, including myself, had been making a stone jetty. I ended up instead on some rocks. As soon as I pulled myself onto a rock, I passed out. Some time later I have a faint recollection of being roughly handled into the bows of a small boat. Then I lost consciousness again.'

The badly-burned Dick Kerr was another of the men thrown into the sea when the picket boat capsized. He, too, decided to make for the shore, but with the north-east wind making a slight chop he kept getting facefuls of water. He turned parallel to the shore, heading towards Scapa Pier, and perhaps as much as two hours later he came upon two dimmed and stationary lights. Despite his injuries he had swum the 1,500 yards to *Pegasus*.

Tom Blundell, too, headed for the cliffs, using a cautious breast stroke. 'I had done a bit of life-saving and reckoned I could make it in my own time,' he explained. 'The oil was thick, but it helped to keep me warm and I had the sense to keep my nose out of it. I eventually came upon a Carley float. There were quite a few men on it and others holding the side, kicking with their feet and trying to propel it towards land. I remember bumping up against one of the men in the water. He must have been hurt because he said: "Mind my bloody arm." When lights came on aboard the *Daisy* there was an argument about whether we should change course for the drifter or continue to make for the shore. Finally we decided the shore was nearer.

'I looked back at the ship. She was practically submerged and I could just make out the blister. *Pegasus* switched on what looked like a signal lantern and swept the water. We still kept kicking, but the float tended to go round in circles. I was still thinking about the baby and my wife. Suddenly, a whaler appeared out of the night and hauled us aboard. All I could say was: "Thank Christ." ' The whaler took them to *Pegasus* where, he thinks, they arrived 'some time around 2.15 or 2.30'.

The water which 'Lofty' Bendell swallowed in the pantry of the POs mess in the hope of bringing death as quickly and painlessly as possible was contaminated with oil and simply made him sick. He retched, vomited, thrashed about – and to his astonishment suddenly found himself shooting to the surface of Scapa Flow. Exactly how it came about is still something of a mystery to him. Sitting in his office in the Radiography Department of Bexhill Hospital he explained: 'I can only think that the bubble of air escaped from the pantry and sucked me out with it.' Up on the surface, shocked by his experience and the close proximity of death, he just swam and swam, almost mechanically. 'I can vaguely remember a light from somewhere sweeping the water and shining on the cliffs,' he said. 'I saw men trying to climb them, only to fall back.' He was eventually picked up by a whaler. Somebody told him he must have been in the water for four hours.

'Gillie' Potter, injured after being hurled out of his hammock and badly lacerated by barnacles, hit the water like a high diver. 'You know how it is,' he said. 'You go down and down and down and then you come up and up and up. The ship was clearly going over and I wanted to get away before she sank. My right arm wasn't helping much – I think I must have torn a muscle – and, as I pulled away, I saw another explosion between the guns of Y turret. The flames went up 40 or 50 feet in the air.'

After this explosion, which is generally thought to have come from a small arms' magazine, he settled down to the task of survival: 'I had the good luck to come across a piece of wreckage. I don't know what it was, but I got my right arm over it and it kept me going. I'm not sure who picked me up in the end, but it was a drifter of some sort. I was completely exhausted. All I could hear was a voice calling: "There's someone over there." They must have heard me splashing. The bows came straight towards me and I saw the tyres on the side, grabbed one of them and hung on. They pulled me out of the water and wiped the oil from my face. Somebody said: "It's old Gillie Potter. Well done, Gillie." They put me up in the bow, alongside a fellow lying on the deck, and when I'd recovered a bit I started talking to him. After a while I realised I was talking to a corpse.'

Aboard the *Daisy* the rescue work went on until there was a grave danger that the overloaded drifter would capsize if an attempt were made to pull any more men out of the water. 'It isn't easy to pull somebody out of clean water if he's on his last legs,' 'Taffy' Davies explained, 'and it becomes a hell of a job when he's all fouled up with oil. When we found anyone there was a rush to one side and the *Daisy* listed heavily. The poor old skipper had 300 or more aboard, some of them badly injured. Some other boats appeared and he decided he had done all he could and set course for the *Pegasus*. There were still voices in the water shouting: "Don't go, *Daisy*." That's the sort of thing you can still remember when you wake out of a bad dream, those voices calling for the *Daisy* not to go.'

Of the 424 officers and men saved out of a complement of more than 1,200, the vast majority were rescued by the *Daisy*, an achievement for which Skipper Gatt was subsequently awarded the DSC. Some doubt exists about what time the cargo of survivors reached *Pegasus*, however. 'Taffy' Davies felt certain – 'as certain as I am that Christmas Day is December 25' – that it was shortly after 0400 hours, early in the morning watch, when he came up the gangway of the seaplane carrier, but it must have been a good deal earlier. ACOS was in a position at 0345 to send a signal to the Admiralty saying: *'Pegasus* reports 300 survivors on board.'

The reaction set in once everybody was in the warmth and safety of the seaplane carrier. Long-service sailors and Marines found themselves shaking uncontrollably while tears coursed

down their oil-streaked faces. As soon as they were given hot
drinks they vomited them up again because of the fuel oil they
had swallowed.

Tom Blundell, one of the earlier arrivals, was already asleep,
having almost lost his precious £13. 1s. of back pay. 'I was
carried up the gangway, taken to a bathroom, stripped and
washed,' he explained. 'They put me in a hammock and I
suddenly thought of my belt. I got up and rushed to the
bathroom. There was a great pile of dirty clothes lying on
the deck, but I rummaged through it until I found my money
belt. The money was still inside it. That was a relief, nearly as
big a relief as being rescued.'

In the meantime, out in the Flow, George White had
recovered consciousness to find himself in the boiler-room
of a drifter with someone patting his face and saying he
appeared to be dead. 'I was covered in oil and dressed in
nothing except my singlet and socks,' he said, 'but a coat had
been placed around my shoulders. My left leg had been torn
badly on the rocks. Bubbles appeared under the oil and, half-
dazed, I sat there, popping the bubbles and watching the blood
run down my leg.

'One of the crew was trying to get me to drink some hot
cocoa. I was terribly sick and brought up oil. That made me
retch again: I never could stand the smell of oil. Eventually we
reached the *Pegasus* where I was given a shower and medical
attention. A little after that a rating asked me if I'd go with him
and identify some bodies laid out on a large deck space. I was
sick again when I saw them. Captain Benn came up shortly after
that and said: "Get that boy out of here."'

Captain Benn had been one of the earliest of all the survivors
to reach *Pegasus* and had already informed ACOS by signal, via
the PWSS on Flotta, that he believed his ship had been
torpedoed. When the *Daisy* eventually arrived, the Marine
corporal of the gangway, told 'Taffy' Davies, who was a chum
of his: 'Your captain sounds a right bastard. He came aboard and

said: "I'm Captain Benn of *Royal Oak*. Fetch me a British warm" Nothing about the poor troops in the water.'

To be fair, expressions about the plight of his men would have served no practical purpose. *Pegasus* had already taken all practical steps to assist *Royal Oak*. Her log reads:

0105	Explosion in *Royal Oak*.
0110	Sent motor boat to *Royal Oak* to investigate.
0115	Three more explosions in *Royal Oak* at intervals of about two minutes [note: the explosions were much closer together than this].
0120	*Royal Oak* observed to have sunk [note: the sinking was actually at 0129]. Sent away all boats to pick up survivors.
0200–0400	Boats returning with survivors.*

Pegasus had also sent a visual signal to ACOS, via the PWSS, at about 0135 saying: 'General. Send all boats', followed by a second signal about half an hour later: '*Royal Oak* is sinking after several internal explosions'. Nobody thought of a U-boat until Captain Benn arrived on board. How could a U-boat get into impregnable Scapa Flow?

John Laughton, who had put down his book, got out of bed and stepped outside his home on the cliffs opposite Scapa Pier after the first explosion, was standing there when the next three occurred. Although his eyes had had time to become accustomed to the dark, he still could not see *Royal Oak*. 'After a while,' he says, 'I began to hear the shouts and cries of the men. It puzzled me, but I came to the conclusion that they must be engaged in some kind of naval manoeuvres.' John Laughton closed his door and went back to bed.

---

* This also points to the arrival of the *Daisy* before 0400 when, with the change of watch, there would have been a different corporal of the gangway.

6

Escape

After the second attack on *Royal Oak*, Lt. Prien decided the time had come to break off the action and make his escape. He can hardly be blamed. He had carried out two attacks resulting in the detonation of four torpedoes; he had no torpedoes in position; and it was a reasonable assumption that he could not hope that his presence would go undetected much longer.

Yet it has seemed to his critics that the log entry dealing with his escape, like the log entry dealing with his abandonment of the approach to the main Fleet anchorage, goes to excessive lengths to justify his decision. Certainly no part of his official story has caused greater controversy. The entry reads:

The harbour springs to life. Destroyers are lit up, more signalling breaks out on every side, and on land, some 200 metres from me, cars roar along the roads. A battleship has been sunk, another damaged and three torpedoes have gone to blazes. All tubes are empty. I decide to withdraw because 1) With my periscopes I cannot conduct night attacks while submerged (see experience on entering), 2) On a bright night I cannot manoeuvre unobserved on a calm sea, 3) I must assume that I was observed by the driver of a car which stopped opposite us, turned around and drove off towards Scapa at high speed, 4) Nor can I go further north, for there, well hidden from my sight, lie the destroyers which were previously dimly distinguishable.

0128 At high speed both engines we withdraw. Everything is simple until we reach Skaildaquoy Point. Then we have more trouble. The tide has fallen and is against us. Engines at slow and dead slow, I attempt to get away. I must leave by the south,

through the narrows, because of the depth of water. Things are again
difficult. Course 058°, slow – 10 knots. I make no progress. At high
speed I pass the southern blockship. The helmsman does magnifi-
cently. High speed ahead both, finally ¾ speed and full ahead all out.
Free of the blockships, ahead a mole. With hard rudder, around it,
and at 0215 hours we are outside again. A pity that only one was
destroyed . . .*

The *Royal Oak* survivors take particular issue with Lt. Prien's
harbour-springs-to-life story. They say he is describing what
he expected to happen, and what ought to have happened,
rather than what did happen. It would, of course, hardly be
human for Lt. Prien to make his exploit sound *easier* than it
was. In addition, there was really quite a lot going on in Scapa
Flow. Looking at the scene from a distance, and being under

---

* 'Jetzt wird es im Hafen lebendig. Zerstörer haben Lichter, aus allen Ecken
wird gemorst, an Land, etwa 200m. von mir ab, brausen Autos über die
Strassen. Es ist ein Schlachtschiff versenkt, ein weiteres beschädigt und drei
Aale hat der Teufel geholt. Alle Rohre sind leer geschossen. Ich entschliesse
mich zum Auslaufen, denn:

'1) Getauchte Angriffe kann ich mit meinen Sehrohren nachts nicht fahren,
siehe Einlauferfahrung, 2) Bei der hellen Nacht kann ich mich bei dem stillen
Wasserspiegel nirgends ungesehen mehr hinbewegen, 3) Ich muss annehmen,
dass mich ein Autofahrer gesehen hat, der querab von uns stehen blieb, kehrt
machte und mit hoher Fahrt nach Scapa zu wegfuhr, 4) Weiter nach Norden
kann ich auch nicht, denn dort liegen, gut gedeckt gegen Sicht durch mich die
vorhin schwach erkannten Zerstörer unter Land.

'0128 Mit 2 x H.F.V. auf Auslaufkurs gegangen. Zunächst ist bis Skaildaquoy Pt. alles einfach. Danach geht es wieder los. Der Wasserstand ist
gefallen, einlaufender Strom. Mit "L.F." und "K.F." versuche ich rauszu-
kommen. Ich muss im Süden durch die Enge wegen der Wassertiefe. Es geht
die Wirbelei wieder los. Mit Kurs 058° und "L.F." – 10sm. stehe ich auf der
Stelle. Mit "H.F." an dem südlichen Sperrschiff vorbeigequält. Der Rudergänger arbeitet vorzüglich. Mit 2 x "H.F.", zuletzt mit "G.F." und "AX.V."
frei von der Schiffssperre, vor mir eine Mole! Mit harten Rudermanövern
auch da noch rum und um 0215 Uhr sind wir wieder draussen. Schade, dass
nur einer vernichtet wurde . . .'

considerable pressure, and believing wrongly that the anchorage had highly sophisticated defences, Lt. Prien may well have thought that Scapa Flow was at last beginning to stir itself and *U-47* would be blown out of the water if she remained any longer.

Royal Oak had switched on a light just before the second attack to examine wood drifting past the ship. After the second attack, torches were used and matches struck on the battleship's deck. Lights of some kind were probably visible aboard *Pegasus* as the rescue operation was mounted. Two lamps were lit aboard the *Daisy*. *Pegasus* swept the sea with a searchlight or signal lantern and exchanged signals with the PWSS on Flotta. Signals may also have been exchanged between the PWSS and other ships in the anchorage where all hands were called in the cruiser *Caledon* at 0200 hours, the cruiser *Colombo* began raising steam at 0215 and the cruiser *Delhi* at 0220. As for the cars roaring about, the only point where *U-47* came close to a road while escaping was during the return passage through Kirk Sound. There may, once again, have been a car or cars on the shore – dances tend to go on late in the Orkneys – but the implication that they were connected in some way with the attack on *Royal Oak* is a false one.

As for Lt. Prien's four reasons for making his escape, while there were no destroyers anchored to the north of *Royal Oak*, there had been a car on the shore as *U-47* passed the village of St Mary's on her way into the anchorage. Of the other two reasons – that he could not operate submerged because it was too dark and he could not operate on the surface because it was too bright – it has been said that they are contradictory. This seems to me to be arguing from the point of view that a statement must be wrong simply because Lt. Prien made it. He would hardly have been late from choice for his rendezvous with slack water in Kirk Sound and an encounter with a vessel provides logical reason for his being behind schedule. There is no indication of the range at which he first saw the ship's navigation lights, but it may well have been far enough away for him to be unable to identify the ship by periscope. As for the visibility, whatever the arguments about it, there was certainly enough light to enable Lt. Prien to carry out two attacks on *Royal Oak* from a range in the neighbourhood of two miles.

It is not clear whether there was any connection between the activity aboard the cruisers *Caledon, Colombo* and *Delhi* and the loss of *Royal Oak*. What is clear is that the account in *Mein Weg Nach Scapa Flow* of patrol boats flitting about, the challenge by a destroyer which turned aside mysteriously, and the dropping of depth charges is a total fabrication.

The story told by some members of *U-47*'s crew that the Scapa defences swept the sky above their heads with search-lights, apparently in the belief that there had been an air raid, was probably inspired by the light shone by *Pegasus* in an attempt to find out what was going on. It is, however, a misinterpretation of the facts. When *U-47* regained the open sea at 0215, it was still believed in Scapa Flow that *Royal Oak* had been destroyed by internal explosion, and the only positive action taken aboard *Iron Duke*, headquarters of ACOS, apart from informing the Admiralty of the loss of the battleship, had been to order all boats to proceed to the *Royal Oak* anchorage at 0155.

It was not, in fact, until more than three quarters of an hour after the escape of *U-47* that the hunt for a suspected submarine began. *Mashona*, one of three Tribal class destroyers to take part, slipped from No. 8 buoy in Gutter Sound at 0303. She was followed by *Somali* at 0328 and *Ashanti* at 0445. The first lieutenant of *Ashanti* at the time was Viscount Jocelyn, now Captain, the Earl of Roden, RN (retired), who retains a very clear picture of the events of that night.

In a letter from his home in Co. Down he told me: 'In those days one or more of the destroyers in harbour were kept at short notice – one hour, I think – but were expected to be under way much sooner than that. The remainder were officially at four hours' notice for sea. This allowed some maintenance on machinery to be carried out, but if none was actually in hand steam could be raised from cold boilers in about two hours. I remember that my captain had dined in another ship that night, which would not have happened had we been one of the emergency destroyers. It is likely therefore that *Ashanti* was at normal notice while the other two were at short notice as duty destroyers.

'The whole feeling in the ship was one of incredulity that a submarine could penetrate Scapa Flow undetected. My captain, who had served for three years in submarines, was firm in his opinion that navigational difficulties would make a submerged approach impossible at night and that it was a reasonable assumption that entries not protected by nets would be sufficiently patrolled to make an undetected approach on the surface impossible as well. The conclusion was therefore that *Royal Oak* had been destroyed by some internal explosion resulting from unstable ammunition or some human error in the handling of it. There had, of course, been several unfortunate precedents of this happening during the 1914 war.

'Scapa Flow was quiet when we slipped from our moorings to start the search and the impression on *Ashanti*'s bridge was that the other two destroyers, which were already in the Flow, shared the feeling that we were wasting our time. This did not, of course, mean any laxity in the search operation, which was conducted most effectively. All three destroyers were from the same Flotilla and were well used to operating together at night. My memory of the weather was that it was a still, clear night.

'Our aim was to detect any submarine and prevent it from leaving the Flow. This involved a pattern of patrol rather than a search for a submarine lying on the sea bed. It did not allow time to assess whether one of the many contacts in a place like Scapa Flow could possibly be a U-boat deserving the ultimate test of a depth charge attack. When daylight came the operation changed in the direction of a search for a bottomed submarine as a result of a Staff appreciation that a U-boat had made the penetration and might still be lying up inside the Flow.'

The hunt was led by Captain (D) aboard *Somali*, later Admiral Sir Gresham Nicholson, KBE, CB, DSO, DSC, RN, who died in the summer of 1975. One of his officers, however, is now Rear-Admiral Maurice Ross, CB, DSC, RN (retired), who confirms Lord Roden's statement that the first reaction to the suggestion that a submarine might have penetrated the anchorage was one of incredulity. 'No one believed it,' he said. Admiral Ross confesses that, after 39 years, his recollection of events is somewhat hazy, but he went on: 'There was *not* an orgy of fireworks soon after the attack and *certainly* not in the neighbourhood of the entrance which *U-47* used. Everyone thought this was effectively blocked and that the only possible entry was through the boom when the gate was open for another ship.'

Out in the open sea, Lt. Prien set a south-easterly course across the Moray Firth and noted – somewhat defensively, it has been suggested – in his log: *'I still have 5 torpedoes for possible use against merchantmen.*** The only British naval vessel anywhere near *U-47* at this time was the destroyer *Matabele*, which had been detached from the patrol with *Southampton* to escort the 750-ton cargo ship *St Clare* from Lerwick in the Shetlands to Aberdeen. They arrived off Aberdeen at 0945, having passed a few miles astern of *U-47* during the night. Lt. Prien and his crew were by then lying on the bottom of the North Sea, some 40 miles north-east of Fraserburgh. *U-47* submerged at 0630 and Lt. Prien wrote: *'The glow from Scapa is still visible for a long time. Apparently they are still dropping depth charges'**

---

* 'Ich habe noch 5 Torpedoes fur evtl. Handelskrieg . . . Der Lichtschein von Scapa ist noch lange zu sehen, anscheinend werfen sie noch Wasserbomben.'

This was not the case. No depth charges had been dropped in Scapa Flow up to that time. Examination of the logs of naval vessels based at Scapa Flow and at Rosyth, or on passage from the Western Approaches, plus all the Admiralty documents relating to the anti-submarine war, also show that no depth charges, which might have been mistaken for Scapa Flow depth charges, were fired in the North Sea at any time during that Saturday. The only recorded U-boat incident involving a British surface vessel was, in fact, an attack carried out by the destroyer HMS *Inglefield* in the Western Approaches at 1530 hours.

In Scapa Flow, and at the Admiralty, it had been a long and confusing night which was to be followed by a long and confusing day. The varied events, signals and suggestions can be most conveniently set out in the form of a log:

0200   ACOS to Admiralty: ROYAL OAK SUNK IN SCAPA FLOW, SERIES OF EXPLOSIONS.

0211   ACOS to Admiralty: NO DETAILS YET AVAILABLE.

0320   ACOS to Admiralty: ONLY EVIDENCE TO DATE THREE EXPLOSIONS. ROYAL OAK WAS LYING OFF EASTERN END OF SCAPA FLOW.

0345   ACOS to Admiralty: PEGASUS REPORTS 300 SURVIVORS ON BOARD.

0500   The tug *St Martin* recovered two bodies in Scapa Flow.

0504   ACOS to Admiralty: REPORT FROM CAPTAIN BENN. HE BELIEVES ROYAL OAK TORPEDOED.

0506   Admiralty to ACOS: CAN IT BE DEFINITELY STATED SINKING NOT DUE TO ENEMY AIRCRAFT?

0620   ACOS to Admiralty: YES.

(In between these two signals the only incident involving the land defences of Scapa Flow took place. At 0530 an oil lamp fell over and caused a fire which burned down an Army observation post on Flotta.)

0641   ACOS to Admiralty: ROYAL OAK PROBABLY SUNK BY TORPEDOES. DIVERS BEING SENT.

0643   Admiralty to ACOS: REQUEST INFORMATION WHEN ROYAL OAK LAST CARRIED OUT FIRINGS, DATE OF LAST AMMUNITIONING AND OILING, WHEN SHE TOOK UP BERTH AND WHETHER SCAPA IS DEFINITELY SUBMARINE-PROOF.

0704   Admiralty to ACOS: NO REFERENCE TO ROYAL OAK TO BE MADE IN PLAIN LANGUAGE UNTIL FURTHER ORDERS. THIS INCLUDES LIST OF SURVIVORS.

0730   *Belfast, Caledon, Cardiff, Colombo* and *Delhi* put to sea from Scapa Flow in quick succession.

0746   ACOS to Admiralty: CONSIDER ROYAL OAK SUNK BY TORPEDOES WITH MAGNETIC PISTOL FIRED BY SUB-MARINE.

0805   *St Martin* recovered a third body.

0829   *Aurora* sailed from Scapa Flow for Loch Ewe.

0905   *St Martin* recovered two more bodies.

0915   *Pegasus* moored alongside the accommodation ship *Voltaire* in Gutter Sound.

0930   *Pegasus* began to disembark survivors and, in the interests of good naval housekeeping, recorded that 'three cork lifebelts, pattern 305, used in the rescue of *Royal Oak* personnel' had not been returned.

1003   C.-in-C., Home Fleet, to ACOS: CONSIDER [THE NETLAYER] GUARDIAN LAYING NETS TO COVER EXITS FROM KIRK, SKERRY AND EAST WEDDEL SOUNDS. USE EVERY POSSIBLE MEANS, INCLUDING AIRCRAFT, TO PREVENT SUBMARINE GETTING OUT AND INFORMING GERMAN ADMIRALTY.

1030   *Ashanti* carried out an attack on a contact in Scapa Flow [these were the first depth charges fired in the anchorage since the loss of *Royal Oak* nine hours earlier].

At the Admiralty a *Statement of Facts So Far Known* was prepared. It read: '12.10.39. German plane over Scapa Flow would have shown *Repulse, Furious* and *Royal Oak* in harbour, besides smaller craft. Dusk, 12/10, *Repulse* and *Furious* sailed, *Repulse* to dock, *Furious* because of possibility of air attack. 2200/12 Men sleeping in gate vessel at Hoxa Gate heard sounds of propellers and reported to watch on deck. Some indication boom nets may have been disturbed, but nothing seen. Presumed submarine entered at this time [note: this theory was later dismissed by the Board of Inquiry]. May have looked for *Repulse* and *Furious* and, having failed to find them, remained on bottom throughout 13th.

'0055/14 Submarine presumably located *Royal Oak* during 13th, fired first torpedo: 20 minutes later two or three more torpedoes, which caused *Royal Oak* to sink. ACOS ordered all ships to raise steam and, except destroyers, they proceeded to sea through Switha Gate. Hoxa Gate closed at this time, not since reopened. Three destroyers now hunting inside the Flow, but ACOS thinks submarine may have escaped through the boom.

1034   C.-in-C., Home Fleet, to ACOS: SEND ALL BIG SHIPS TO SEA . . . BELFAST TO PORT A (Loch Ewe).

1109   ACOS to Admiralty: REQUEST INSTRUCTIONS AS TO WITHHOLDING CIVILIAN TELEPHONIC COMMUNICATION WITH MAINLAND.

1133   C.-in-C., Home Fleet, to ACOS: POSSIBILITY . . . THAT SUBMARINE ENTERED THROUGH KIRK SOUND AT SLACK HIGH WATER AT ABOUT 2315 AND WILL ATTEMPT TO GET OUT THE SAME WAY TODAY OR TOMORROW.

1155   Admiralty to ACOS: YOUR 1109/14. FOLLOWING HAS BEEN GIVEN TO PRESS [the official announcement of the loss *of Royal Oak* followed].

1255   *Mashona* attacked a contact in the Flow.

1323   *Ashanti* attacked a contact in the Flow.

1325 ACOS to Admiralty: SEARCHES BY DESTROYERS, MINESWEEPERS AND AIRCRAFT CARRIED OUT.

1327 *Somali* attacked a contact in the Flow.

1505 An expression of condolence from the King of Norway was transmitted to the Admiralty by the Naval Attaché in Oslo.

2046 Admiralty to ACOS: GERMAN OFFICIAL ANNOUNCEMENT. THEY ARE WITHOUT CONFIRMATION FROM ANY GERMAN SOURCE. FROM THIS IT WOULD APPEAR THAT SUBMARINE IS STILL IN HARBOUR.

2233 ACOS to Admiralty: DIVERS EXAMINED PORT SIDE AND FLAT BOTTOM OF ROYAL OAK, FOUND NO DAMAGE YET.

2253 Admiralty to ACOS: DO NOT HESITATE TO USE SEARCHLIGHTS FOR HUNTING SUBMARINE TONIGHT.

The belief that a U-boat was still trapped inside Scapa Flow died hard. As late as Wednesday, October 18, the day after Lt. Prien's safe return to Germany and his broadcast, the C.-in-C., Home Fleet, sent a signal timed 1858 containing the somewhat bizarre advice: SUGGEST SEARCH ALONGSIDE ROYAL OAK, STARBOARD SIDE: SUBMARINE MAY HAVE BEEN PINNED DOWN WHEN ROYAL OAK SANK. It was not until Sunday, October 22, that the destroyer search inside the Flow was finally abandoned.

In the interval, Lt. Prien had completed a voyage home that passed without any incident of great importance. On the night of Saturday, October 14, *U-47* surfaced at 1935 and set off on a course of 180°. Lt. Prien explained in his log: *This course was chosen in the hope that we might catch a ship inshore, and to avoid U-20.* * The shape of the Scottish coastline meant, however, that he actually put a progressively greater distance between himself

---

* 'Dieser Kurs wird gewahlt in der HoShung, vielleicht noch einen zu erwischen unter der Küste und um *U-20* auszuweichen.'

and land once he had passed Peterhead. In the course of the night *U-47* was in radio communication with Germany and Admiral Dönitz noted in his war diary: 'Received from *U-47* the following message: "Operation carried out as planned. *Royal Oak* sunk: *Repulse* damaged."'

When Lt. Prien submerged at 0600 on the Sunday morning, he was in a position (56°20′N, 0°40′W) some 78 miles off the Bass Rock at the entrance to the Firth of Forth. At this point, Lt. Prien's log makes another reference to depth charges which has, with the passing years, given rise to the myth that *U-47* was the object of the attack although Lt. Prien's entry makes it perfectly plain that this was not the case. The entry reads: *From 1000, depth charges were fired from time to time in the far distance. Thirty-two were definitely counted. Therefore I remain lying on the bottom until dusk.* *

This account tallies precisely with Admiralty records. At 1000 the destroyer HMS *Afridi* carried out a depth charge attack on a target, subsequently identified as a wreck teeming with pollack, to the north-east of the Bass Rock. *Afridi* and the destroyer HMS *Woolston* carried out further attacks in the Firth of Forth between 1130 and 1400. More depth charges were fired by HMS *Valorous* in the same area at 1414. In addition, the destroyer HMS *Broke* carried out an attack off Blyth, Northumberland, just over a hundred miles from *U-47*, at 1615. All of the depth charges dropped in these operations would have been audible at those distances to the crew of *U-47*, which eventually surfaced at 1823 and set a south-easterly course for home.

At that time, back in Germany, the Luftwaffe was busy making preparations for what is sometimes referred to in Britain as 'The Forth Bridge Raid'. This is a misnomer. The target was

* 'Ab 1000 Uhr werden in grosser Entfernung von Zeit zu Zeit Wasserbomben geworfen. Es werden mit Sicherheit 32 Bomben gezahlt. Ich bleibe deshalb bis zur Abenddämmerung auf Grund liegen.'

not the Forth Bridge, despite its importance as a means of communication, but a ship – *Repulse*, which Lt. Prien had ostensibly left crippled in Scapa Flow 40 hours earlier.

The following morning, while *U-47* lay safely on the Dogger Bank in the middle of the North Sea, the telephone rang in the office of Captain Helmut Pohle at Westerland on the island of Sylt. Captain Pohle, C.O. of I/KG30 bomber squadron, had been one of the disappointed pilots involved a week earlier in the *Gneisenau* foray which had lured the Home Fleet out of Scapa Flow just as Lt. Prien was leaving on his mission. Now there was more bad news for him. At the other end of the telephone was Lt.-Gen. Hans Jeschonnek, Luftwaffe Chief of Staff, with some final, and very definite, instructions about the procedure to be followed on the Forth raid, scheduled for that afternoon.

Hitler had given a personal order that the battlecruiser* spotted in the Forth by aerial reconnaissance was not to be attacked if she had entered dock because, still hoping for peace, he did not wish to risk bombs falling on British soil and killing civilians.

This is the account of the raid which appears in the *Luftwaffe War Diaries* by Cajus Bekker: 'At 1100 on October 16, I/KG30's bomber squadron took off. By 1215 they had reached the outer estuary of the Forth and started to push inland . . . As Pohle flew at the head of his scattered formation, Edinburgh came into view below. For the first time since the war began a German bomber unit was flying over the United Kingdom. There was the great bridge separating the outer and inner Firth of Forth and, immediately beyond it on the north bank, the docks of Rosyth naval base.

* There seems to have been some confusion in German minds about the battlecruiser. The German navy had identified the ship correctly as the *Repulse* while the Luftwaffe apparently thought the target was the *Hood*.

'At once Pohle spotted the ship that he had come to sink, distinguished by its length and much greater width from the much smaller ships around. It could only be the *Hood*, but she was no longer at sea, but in dock – or, rather, in the sluice gate leading to it . . . "She was a sitting target," Pohle reported, "but orders robbed us of our prize." '

That report had to be made very much later, however, for the Forth raid was Captain Pohle's last mission of the war. Robbed of *Repulse* because of her position, he turned his attention to the cruiser *Southampton*, recently arrived after her patrol off the Shetlands. As Captain Pohle dived on *Southampton* at 400 m.p.h., the cabin roof of his Ju88 dive-bomber sheered off. That was only the beginning of his misfortunes. The thousand-pound bomb which he launched at the cruiser from 3,000 feet struck its target but failed to explode, and as Captain Pohle turned away he was set upon by three Spitfires. Over East Lothian, with his aircraft badly damaged and his radio operator, rear gunner and observer dead, he decided to put down in the sea: 'We were finished. I spied a trawler steaming north and thought perhaps I could reach it.' He crash-landed in the water, lost consciousness and woke up five days later in a Scottish hospital.

U-47 tied up at Wilhelmshaven at 1144 on the Tuesday morning. It was an euphoric occasion. Hitler had already promoted Commodore Dönitz to Admiral; awarded Lt. Prien the Iron Cross, First Class, and his crew the Iron Cross, Second Class; and given Grand Admiral Erich Raeder, C.-in-C. of the German Navy, authority to intensify the U-boat war. He had also ordered that the entire crew of *U-47* be flown to Berlin where Lt. Prien was to receive the coveted Knights' Cross of the Iron Cross on their behalf.

Both Grand Admiral Raeder and Admiral Dönitz were at Wilhelmshaven in person to greet Lt. Prien and hear from his own lips the details of his mission. Admiral Dönitz later recorded in his war diary: 'It is obvious from the report that the operation has been carried out with enormous courage and competence . . .'

In the afternoon, Lt. Prien and his crew were flown first to Kiel for their uniforms, then to Berlin to be received by the Führer. From Tempelhof Airport they drove in open cars through streets lined with waving, cheering throngs. After he and his crew had been received by Hitler at his Chancellery, Lt. Prien was introduced to German and foreign correspondents by Hitler's Press chief, Dr Otto Dietrich, who – the American correspondent William Shirer notes in his book *Berlin Diary* – 'kept cursing the English and calling Churchill a liar'. Then it was on to an evening at the theatre where the heroes of Scapa Flow were joined by a delighted Dr Goebbels, the Propaganda Minister.

The delight of Dr Goebbels was understandable. At the time a great deal of his energy was being devoted to making maximum capital out of the war at sea and *U-47* could hardly have served him better. It is therefore not surprising that the hand of the propagandist, as well as the genesis of some of the myths surrounding Lt. Prien's exploit, can be detected in the story written for *Der Angriff*, Dr Goebbel's own news-paper, by a correspondent who had flown to Berlin with Lt. Prien:

'We are sitting among the crew of the U-boat which has returned to its home base after its successful voyage to Scapa Flow. The crew are still full of the adventure. Lt. Prien, commander of the triumphant U-boat, tries to describe to us in a speech the voyage and what it was like in the British war anchorage of Scapa Flow . . .

'Questioned about the penetration of Scapa Flow, he said frankly: "The war has already lasted six weeks. On all the trips* I have made in my U-boat up till now, I have not caught a

* One prior to the Scapa Flow mission.

glimpse of a single enemy warship. It was the wish of the whole crew to have just one British warship in the sights of our torpedo tubes. This was not just what I wanted. Every officer and every man wanted it as well. However, as it is not possible to meet a British warship on the high seas today, the only remaining possibility was to penetrate a British harbour . . ."'

Scapa Flow, it was explained, had been chosen to avenge the internment of the German Fleet after the first World War and its subsequent scuttling. 'The commander then went on to speak about details of the voyage: "It was as bright as day because of the Northern Lights on a scale I have never before encountered in my service at sea . . . After we had penetrated the harbour, my first concern was to ensure that we were not discovered before we found the targets hidden from us. To the north, directly ahead of me, I saw the silhouettes of two battleships, the target which every U-boat sailor hopes for. So, onto them! Torpedo tubes ready! Crew at action stations!"

'While Lt. Prien was speaking these words, the faces of his crew, standing around him, shone with pride over the memory of what lay behind them. All want to contribute to describing the hours and minutes which they will never forget as long as they live. Nobody speaks of himself, each tries to praise the heroic deeds of his comrades.

'The commander of the U-boat finally came to the eventful climax: "When we were at the right distance from the two battleships, the torpedo tubes were prepared for firing. Now it's all up to the technicians. And they do the necessary. The first torpedo struck the battleship with two funnels that was furthest away from us, the second torpedo struck the nearer one . . . The northern ship – it looked like the *Repulse* – was not sunk but was, without any doubt at all, seriously damaged. The bow of the ship sank deep in the water immediately.

'"The effect of the second torpedo was peculiar . . ."' Lt. Prien then went on to describe the violent end of *Royal Oak* with cascades of water, flames 'in all the colours of the rainbow', chunks of the battleship flying through the air. 'These,' he explained, 'were parts of the funnel, the mast and the bridge-work.' The story went on: 'Finally, we asked the commander of the successful U-boat about the impression the reception given to him and his crew on their return had made on them. Lt. Prien replied: "On my arrival . . . I became conscious for the first time of the deep interest the German people had taken in what was, for us U-boat men, a routine voyage. I am convinced that my crew has also been inspired to do everything they can to bring this war to an early, honourable and victorious end." '

Back in England that same afternoon the atmosphere in the House of Commons had been considerably more sombre when Mr Churchill, who had been brought back into favour as First Lord of the Admiralty at the start of the war, rose to make his preliminary statement about the loss of *Royal Oak*. 'The *Royal Oak* was sunk at anchor by a U-boat in Scapa Flow approximately at 1.30 a.m. on October 14,' he said. 'It is still a matter of conjecture how the U-boat penetrated the defences of the harbour. When we consider that, during the whole course of the last war, this anchorage was found to be immune from such attacks on account of the obstacles imposed by the currents and the net barrages, this entry by a U-boat must be considered as a remarkable exploit of professional skill and daring.

'A Board of Inquiry is now sitting at Scapa Flow to report upon all that occured, and anything that I say must be subject to revision in the light of their conclusions. It appears probable that the U-boat fired a salvo of torpedoes at the *Royal Oak*, of which only one hit the bow. This muffled explosion was at the time attributed to internal causes, and what is called the inflammable store, where the kerosene and other such materials are kept, was flooded. Twenty minutes later, the U-boat fired three or more torpedoes, and these, striking in quick succession, caused the ship to capsize and sink.

'She was lying at the extreme edge of the harbour and therefore many officers and men were drowned before rescue could be organized from other vessels. Serious as this loss is, it does not affect the margin of security in heavy vessels, which remains ample. Meanwhile, an intensive search of the anchorage has not yielded any results. It is clear, however, that after a certain time the harbour can be pronounced clear as any U-boat would have to rise to the surface for air or perish. All necessary measures are being taken to increase the precautions which in the late war proved effectual.'

Up in Scapa Flow, the day had brought two German air raids and another set-back for the Royal Navy. In the first raid, *Iron Duke*, the partly-demilitarised veteran of Jutland which served as headquarters for ACOS and his staff, was holed on the port side, took an immediate list of 12 degrees and had to be beached near Lyness.

The two raids had a shattering effect on the *Royal Oak* survivors, who were being kept at Scapa Flow pending the Board of Inquiry. In response to protests the Admiralty agreed that, for the sake of their morale, the vast majority of them could be transferred by minesweeper to Thurso on the mainland. They looked a motley collection of men – some with white caps, some with black caps, some with no caps at all . . . some in boilersuits, some in fishermen's jerseys and ill-fitting trousers . . . some wearing seaboots, some gym shoes – when they arrived a few hours later to be billeted on hospitable local families.

News of the sinking of *Iron Duke* was brought to Vincent Marchant, still recovering in the cottage hospital at Kirkwall from his long swim, by a 15-year-old ward maid, with whom he had struck up a friendship. 'She had never been out of the islands,' he told me 'and she used to like to sit on my bed and ask me questions about England – had I been to London, had I seen Piccadilly, that sort of thing. She was a nice girl – I saw her again a couple of years ago when a lot of us went up to Scapa Flow for a remembrance ceremony over the wreck of *Royal Oak* – and she came in on the day of the air raids and said "The Germans have sunk a battleship."

'I said: "I know, luv, I was on it."

'She said: "Not the *Royal Oak*, another battleship, the *Iron Duke*."

'I thought: "Bloody hell, if it goes on like this we won't have a Fleet left by Christmas." '

7

Board of Inquiry

The three members of the Board of Inquiry appointed by the Admiralty caught the Euston–Thurso train on the night of Monday, October 16. Their president was the splendidly-named Admiral Sir Reginald Aylmer Ranfurly Plunkett-Ernle-Erle-Drax, KGB, DSO, RN, second son of the 17th Baron Dunsany, and he had the assistance of Vice-Admiral Robert Raikes, CB, CVO, DSO, RN, an experienced submariner, and Captain Gerard Muirhead-Gould, DSO, RN.

During the voyage from Scrabster, the port of Thurso, to Lyness, Admiral Raikes appeared on the bridge of the minesweeper *Seagull* where Harry Smith of Portland, then an Acting Yeoman of Signals, was on duty. 'I heard a fair amount of the conversation,' he recalls. 'Admiral Raikes most certainly did not hold then with the opinion that it was a U-boat job.' If this was the case, his mind was changed for him in the course of the next week, during which the Board heard formal testimony from 31 witnesses – 19 survivors from *Royal Oak*, ACOS and six members of his staff, two civilians and three ratings from the boom defence vessel *Dragonet* who were questioned about propeller noises heard on the night of October 11–12. In addition to verbal evidence, the Board had at its disposal the written answers to a questionaire filled in by survivors, a history of the Scapa Flow defences, two 1939 surveys of the eastern entrances, details of the action to be taken in the event of an enemy surface vessel or submarine penetrating the anchorage and three newspaper cuttings containing Lt. Prien's story.

The following account of the proceedings before the Board has been edited to some extent to avoid repetition of survivors' individual experiences and to excise irrelevant testimony, arising from the fact that, at that stage, nobody could be sure whether a U-boat had penetrated one of the eastern entrances, followed a ship in through a boom, or even slipped around the side of a boom.

The first witness was Skipper Gatt, who was questioned briefly about whether it had been the practice of German trawlers to enter Scapa Flow by the 'blocked' eastern entrances between the wars. He agreed that it had, and added that he himself had made the passage as a deckhand on a British trawler. For his experience of the actual sinking, the Board relied on a report written in his own hand 24 hours after his gallant rescue work. It ended with the postscript: 'One item I forgot to mention was that there was no panic and the men behaved wonderfully in the circumstances.'

Skipper Gatt was followed by Captain Benn, who was to be recalled several times in the course of the hearing. On this first appearance he was asked: 'Have you any personal knowledge of whether there were columns of water that might have indicated torpedo explosions outside?'

He replied: 'Only from what I have heard afterwards. I have subsequently been told, although I did not notice it myself when standing on the forecastle before going below, that the forecastle deck forward was quite wet. The whole of what I saw of the rest of the upper deck was quite dry. Further information I gained from men whom I questioned is that a spout of water was seen to go up with the first explosion. Also that the second or third explosion drenched the air defence position, which is on the foremast above and abaft the compass platform.'

Commander Edmund Hopkinson, the Boom Defence Officer, next answered some questions about boom openings on October 12 and 13.* Then . . .

'Please give us the times of high water at Hoxa on the night of October 13–14' – 'I have not got it for that day, but next day it was 1158.'

'It has been stated by the First Lord that *Royal Oak* was sunk by a submarine. Assuming this to be established, at what entrance do you think it most probable that the submarine came in?' – 'Through Holm Sound.'

'Is the strength of the tide at Hoxa as shown on the chart correct or are you exposed to stronger than that?' – 'Considerably stronger than that are experienced. The tides are very inconsistent. At spring tides the tide runs between two or three knots and varies considerably in direction in that sometimes one section of net will be bowed to the flood and the adjacent section will be sagged to the ebb. At times you get a lateral tide and you see the trots and nets turn round sideways. There are also considerable eddies.'

The Board then called Thomas Mackenzie, chief salvage officer of Metal Industries Ltd., whose experience with the German Fleet, scuttled after the first World War, had given him a profound knowledge of the Scapa tides and entrances. In 1939 he had also carried out a survey of the entrances on the Admiralty's behalf.

'I believe you have long experience of working drifters through all these passages' – 'Yes sir, a lot.'

'What is the average draught of drifters using these waters?' – 'We have taken drifters and trawlers up to 12ft.6in. draught.'

'Will you please tell us the passage a vessel of 12ft.6in. draught, or perhaps up to 15ft., could pass?' – 'Ahead [note:

---

* All of the times given by Commander Hopkinson coincide with the ship movements detailed in Chapter III. On October 13, for instance, *Furious, Fearless* and *Foxhound* sailed at 0140. According to Commander Hopkinson the boom was open from 0126 until 0228.

to the north] of the [blockship] *Soriano* in Kirk Sound. I took the anchor of the *Soriano* and stretched it right inshore until my tug was aground, but I would not say it was completely sealed. Ahead [note: to the south] of the [blockship] *Thames:* between *Thames* and Lamb Holm, there is a definite passage about 400 feet wide and with a depth of four to four and a half fathoms (*24–27ft.*) at low water. Of course, there is a very strong tide running up to 10 knots, but there is slack water of 15 minutes.'

'Then for the defence of that passage I gather we rely on the tide rather than on the complete blockage' – 'Yes, I think that is right.'

'Is there [another] channel a submarine could come through?' – 'Yes, through Hoy Sound.'

'Is it your opinion a submarine could quite easily enter through Hoy Sound?' – 'I think a submarine could. The passage is much easier than Kirk Sound. It is regularly navigated by Coast of Scotland steamers with a draught of 16ft.'

'The gap you refer to at Kirk Sound. Would it be correct to say that the tide runs up to 10 knots to within half an hour each side of high and low water?' – 'Yes, that is correct, but the velocity of the tides decreases slowly from about half an hour before high water and low water and attains its maximum velocity about half an hour later.'

The next witness to be called was Admiral Sir Wilfred French, ACOS.

'Will you please tell us what you consider caused the loss of *Royal Oak?*' – 'A submarine that fired four or five torpedoes.'

'Do you think there is any doubt that a submarine did enter the Flow and attack her?' – 'I think there is a possible doubt because it has not yet been established that she was sunk by torpedoes.'

'Do you expect to get a further report from divers tomorrow or shortly?' – 'As soon as I can take them off *Iron Duke.*'

'Do you think the divers' reports will make this point quite clear?' – 'Yes, I do.'

Left. The *U-47* sailing from a French port. Prien is on the right.

Below. HMS *Royal Oak* during the First World War at full speed showing her guns at full elevation. (Imperial War Museum)

Construction of the Churchill Barriers. This is number 4 Barrier, between South Ronaldsay and Burray. The lower arm in the centre of the photograph now blocks Kirk Sound which *U-47* used to enter Scapa Flow. (SCRAN)

HMS *Royal Oak* at anchor in Scapa Flow in 1939. The torpedoes struck amidships and aft. (Imperial War Museum)

The *U-47*.

Land was only 1000 yards away but few survivors reached its safety. The plaque on the buoy reads: 'This marks the wreck of HMS *Royal Oak* and the grave of her crew. Respect their resting place. Unauthorised diving prohibited.'

Günther Prien and Oberleutnant Hans Wessel receiving congratulations from the builders of *U-47*. (SCRAN)

Günther Prien being honoured by Hitler, October 1939. (SCRAN)

Günther Prien being greeted by Vice Admiral Doenitz on 13 December 1939.
(Imperial War Museum)

Part of one of the torpedoes which hit HMS *Royal Oak* on 14 October 1939. (SCRAN)

'Do you think the submarine got out again and, if so, how?' – 'There is absolutely no evidence anywhere that a submarine has got out of the Flow, only the evidence that so far we have completely failed to locate it. There is one position which has been depth-charged, but has not yet been properly examined by divers.'

'Do you feel confident you would have had a report of it if a submarine passed out after sinking *Royal Oak?*' – 'No. I think there was a period of about two or three hours after the sinking of *Royal Oak* when a submarine might have got out without being observed.'

'Where would you expect her to get out in that case?' – 'The Kirk Sound.'

'Can you give us the time of high water in Kirk Sound and the time of slack water on that night?' – 'I think it was 1200]note: the witness clearly meant midnight] and slack water about half an hour each side.'

'From your knowledge of this base, is it your opinion that Cromarty, Rosyth or any other North Sea base can be made more secure than Scapa for the Home Fleet?' – 'I should say undoubtedly yes because, in the past, we have always relied on the psychological effect of the varying tides of the Pentlands which, as a matter of fact, are not so big a bogey to those who know [them] as people make out.'

'What improvements in the defence against submarines and surface craft are to be carried out at an early date?' – 'A double anti-submarine net at Hoxa, loop minefields with warning loops at Hoxa and Switha. A blockship is being sunk in Kirk Sound to close the existing gap. These are Admiralty measures. In addition, locally I have instructed the Boom Defence Officer to extend all his booms so as to close the existing gaps except where such gaps are really essential for small craft traffic, and it is proposed to have watches on these gaps at night' . . .

'How many service trawlers have you usually had since the war started to patrol the booms?' – 'Since the Fleet has taken to using Port A [Loch Ewe] and another port, I have had only four.'

'What number of yachts and drifters do you consider should be permanently available to make the watch effective on all entrances?' – 'Ten.'

'What patrol vessels were operating on the night of Friday, October 13, and where were they?' – 'There were patrol vessels at Hoxa and Hoy booms, no others.'

'Had there been an air reconnaissance before [the sinking]?' – 'Yes, two days before.'

Captain Benn was recalled and asked about the position of the inflammable store where the first explosion was thought to have taken place. He replied: 'It is the fourth compartment. I think it is about 40 feet from forward.' After this brief reappearance he was succeeded by Commander Reginald Nichols, *Royal Oak*'s senior executive officer.

'How much of the [anchor] cable gear was broken away by the [first] explosion?' – 'All the slips on both port and starboard cables.'

'Have you any theory as to why exactly the slips parted?' – 'I believe that cast iron is likely to part under stress such as caused by an explosion.'

Commander Nichols was then asked about the water-tightness of the ship at the time of the sinking. He replied that the Commander-in-Chief had issued 'an order or a signal or a memorandum – I can't remember which – pointing out the desirability of keeping living spaces well ventilated during these long darken-ship nights.'

'What height above the water would be the lowest line of scuttles that were open?' – 'I should say about 10 feet.'

Captain Benn, recalled again, was asked: 'Can you estimate, even roughly, how many men were not saved who were in the water when the ship sank?' – 'No, sir.'

'Were you satisfied with the general water-tightness of *Royal Oak*?' – 'Personally, I was not.'

'Will you amplify that?' – 'The Ventilation and Watertight

Compartments Officer, Lt. Moore, who took a tremendous interest in this part of the ship's organisation, told me more than once that he feared that the ship would not stand up to one torpedo under the bottom. His reasons so far as I could understand them were that the ship was old, some of the ventilating trunks had no valves in them and fractures in various trunks would flood adjacent compartments. The ship had a few days previously been to sea in bad weather and this had happened the starboard fresh-water tank was found to have salt-water in it, and, on being emptied, it was found that certain rivets were leaking and an overlap in the ship's sideplates also leaked. The marines' messdeck had got water into it through a ventilator which had been carried away . . . and on arrival in harbour it was found that the implement store immediately below this messdeck had about two feet of water in it . . .'

Next came Engineer Commander John Renshaw.

'What was the condition of the oil fuel tanks when the ship was torpedoed?' – '. . . The ship was 90 per cent full of oil fuel except for the inner tanks in A boiler-room, which were in use, but they were nearly full.'

'Can you say if there were any internal explosions?' – 'I cannot say.'

'Do you know of any evidence that columns of water were seen to rise on the starboard side of the ship or to have fallen on the ship?' – 'I understand other witnesses saw this, but I did not.'

A statement by Lt.-Cdr. Richard Gregoy, *Royal Oak*'s navigator, was then read into the evidence: 'When the first explosion occurred I was undressing in my cabin [in the bridge structure]. Time, 0104. I went to the flag deck and was informed the explosion was right under the bows. A large column of water had been shot up above the forecastle level and the cable had run out . . . [After the next explosions] I went over the side where I sat and undressed. Very shortly afterwards the ship turned turtle but I managed to keep pace with her and fetched up on the ship's bottom. Subsequently three other men and myself climbed back again onto the bilge keel where we remained for some seven to 10 minutes [arrived on keel at 0133]. During this time the ship remained steady, settling very slowly. I walked some way forward but the hull appeared intact. I took to the water about 0140 by which time there was about eight feet of the blister (apart from the bilge keel) still above water.'

'From whom did you get the information about the column of water thrown up by the first explosion?' – 'From the signalman of the watch.'

'Please repeat all he told you' – 'He stated that a large column of water had been thrown up in the bows, and, on being questioned, he said he thought it was much bigger than could have been caused by the port anchor falling.'

'Did all the explosions seem to you equally violent?' – 'Allowing for the fact that I was further from the last than I was from the second and third, I think they were all about the same.'

'Was it a very dark night?' – 'When one's eyes grew accustomed to it, it was comparatively light. Men swimming could be seen for about 70 yards.'

Sub-Lt. Anthony Pearman, the next witness, was questioned about a written statement he had made describing how the second and third explosions had caused a shower of water to drench the after part of the compass platform, and a sheet of orange flame, thought to be the cordite flame venting around the funnel case. He was then replaced by Surgeon-Commander George Ritchie.

'How many persons have you seen who are definitely suffering effects of poisonous or other gases?' – 'One, sir, the Pay Commander.'

'To what extent has he been affected?' – 'Moderately badly.'

'Can you identify the nature of the gas?' – 'I think it was cordite fumes.'

'The effect produced might have been caused by cordite or the fumes of some other explosive?' – 'Yes, sir.'

'Was there any evidence of carbon monoxide?' – 'He was not affected by carbon monoxide.'

Captain Benn was recalled again.

'What SOS signals were made from the ship?' – 'The commander ordered a signal to be made to *Pegasus*. When I got to *Pegasus* some time later and I had consulted with one or two officers, I felt very strongly of the opinion that the ship must have been torpedoed. I had an immediate signal made to ACOS to inform him of my opinion so that counter action could be taken at once. This was followed by an amplifying signal and a further signal.'

'Please give us your remarks on rescue work, mentioning speed, efficiency and any point of special interest' – 'A great deal of rescue work was carried out by the drifter *Daisy II* who was alongside the port side of the ship and got clear after the fourth explosion. The remainder was carried out so far as I know by boats from *Pegasus*, assisted, I believe, by a drifter sent over by the King's Harbour Master, Lyness. I believe also that some drifters which were alongside Scapa Pier, about one and a half miles away, when *Royal Oak* went down also carried out rescue work . . . The skipper of the *Daisy II* and his crew did everything possible to get men aboard and into warm positions. The action of *Pegasus* appears to me to be very prompt and commendable. They appear to have sent boats away at once. Not only did they do this, but they sent blankets away in boats and they appear to have made every possible arrangement, giving up everything in the ship to the care and attention to men rescued. They were simply magnificent. When in the water I saw a searchlight burning which I imagine came from *Pegasus*.'

'Were any other searchlights used?' – 'Not as far as I know. No other ship was near.'

'Have you the impression that a large proportion of the men in the water were subsequently saved?' – 'I have an impression that very many of the men who went over the side were saved.'

'Please tell us how you left the ship.' – 'After the fourth

explosion . . . I moved over to the port guardrails with some difficulty. I sat on them for a moment or two and had a good look at the ship and started to walk up the ship's side: the ship must by then have heeled over to more than 90 degrees. I think I only went a very few feet when the ship appeared to capsize very quickly. A large number of men came falling down the ship's side past me, and I slipped down until I fetched up on something in the water, which I now imagine must have been the guardrails. My next impression was that the keel of the ship was well over my head and falling on top of me. At that moment, some force threw me straight up the side of the ship and eventually a few yards away when I started to swim.'

Commander Nicholls was now recalled to be questioned on the subject of signals.

'Please tell us what you know of any SOS signals from *Royal Oak*.' – 'As soon as I got onto B gun deck after the fourth explosion, I hailed the flag deck and told them to make a general signal on their projector to send all boats. The reply I got back was that all power had failed.'

'Had you a rocket on the bridge, ready for firing, or Very lights?' – 'I cannot say, and, unfortunately, it did not occur to me to order their use.'

'Can you say what visual signal from ships in the harbour would have been regarded as an urgent distress signal?' – 'There would have been nothing more than the normal international signals for a ship in distress.'

'Were any such signals made from *Pegasus*?' – 'I saw none, but I know she made a general signal to send all boats to *Royal Oak*.'

'Did *Pegasus* promptly switch on a searchlight and was it helpful?' – 'I saw her burning a searchlight soon after I was in the water, but it was of no assistance as far as I know.'

The next testimony was provided by Commander Oswald Frewen, who explained that he had been 'appointed in March as Senior Naval Officer and King's Harbour Master, Scapa, with a view to the development of the base'.

'Which entrances to Scapa Flow are you responsible for the closing, or defence, of?' – 'I am not personally responsible for any of them, only to point out to the Rear-Admiral and Commanding Officer, Coast of Scotland (COCOS), and later to ACOS, which gaps in my opinion are dangerous.'

'Have you made any written reports on the subject?' – 'No, sir. The matter was already in hand when I was appointed.'

'What verbal representations have you made on the subject since you got here?' – 'When I got here the *Soriano* had already been laid in Kirk Sound . . . and the *Naja* had been laid in Water Sound. I understood that three or four more blocksbips were to be laid by Metal Industries, who had laid the other two and were going to purchase the ships privately and lay them. Later there was some question of reversing the whole arrangement and laying no more. HMS *Scott* came up and carried out a survey as a result of which the Rear-Admiral and Commanding Officer, Coast of Scotland, recommended that four more blockships be put down. I then heard no more blockships were going to be put down as Their Lordships were satisfied the Sounds were . . . too dangerous for navigation. When Admiral French came up, about June, I think, I took him out and in again through both Skerry and Kirk Sounds in a boom defence picket boat, and, in view of Mr Mackenzie of Metal Industries offering to bring in a reasonably sized tramp through either of these Sounds, I understand that Admiral French reported to the Admiralty and obtained sanction for two more block-ships.'

'Would you consider two more sufficient or would you prefer four?' – 'Since the *Soriano* we have placed the *Cape Ortegal*, which, in my opinion, makes Skerry Sound absolutely safe. We are today [note: October 21] laying the *Lake Neuchatel*, which, if it is successful, will make Kirk Sound absolutely safe. I am not prepared to say that East Weddel or Water Sounds are 100 per cent safe.'

'Do you mean you cannot guarantee that the *Royal Oak* episode might not be repeated by a German submarine entering one of these passages?' – 'I think it would be very, very difficult, but I think it is possible.'

'If the *Lake Neuchatel* completely blocks the south gap in Kirk Sound, are you satisfied that a small submarine with modern wirecutters could not get through to the northward of *Soriano*?' – 'I think it is a possibility.'

'Would it then be wise to have a blockship in this position?' – 'I think the passage north of the *Soriano* would scarcely require a blockship if a ship's cable rather than the present five and a half inch ship's wire were used between the bows of the *Soriano* and low-water mark.'

'Do you know if before October 13 there were any coast watchers to watch the gaps between the blockships and the shore?' – 'I think there was no continuous watch, and I under-stand that when a ship grounded on one of the northern islands a Metal Industries tug proceeded straight through Kirk Sound during the night on the way out there and returning, and she was not reported by anyone. She drew about 13ft.6in.'

'What was the state of the tide when the tug passed through?' – 'She passed out near low water.'

'Do you know if it was a dark night?' – 'Not very dark, sir.'

'If it be assumed that a small German submarine drawing about 12½ft. entered Scapa on the surface on the night of October 13, please state all the different places at which you think she might have entered.' – 'In view of the open space south of the (blockship) *Thames* in Kirk Sound, I would not have thought that any submarine would have bothered with any of the other entrances . . .'

'We have heard it stated that a small vessel could point herself at a narrow passage, stop her engines and be swept through by the tide without risk of hitting either side. Have you heard this stated?' – 'I have heard it with reference to the Pentland Firth, but not with regard to the eastern Sounds.'

'We have heard it stated that, in recent years, German trawlers have passed constantly in and out of Scapa through

Hoy and Kirk Sounds. If German submarine officers had come in these vessels, would you say that this would make it much easier for them to bring a submarine in under war conditions?' – 'Yes, sir, definitely.'

In addition to the gaps between the blockship *Soriano* and the northern shore of Kirk Sound, and the blockship *Thames* and the southern shore of Kirk Sound, there was a gap between the blockships themselves. Commander Frewen was asked: 'What is the distance between *Thames* and *Soriano* and the approximate depth at high water?'

He replied: 'There is a gap of 145 feet with five and a half fathoms (33ft.) at high water,' and went on to explain that the gap between the blockships was protected by 'a taut 12in. hemp for moral effect' and an arrangement of seven-inch and six-inch wires attached to seven-and-a-half-ton anchors.

The last witness but one was Commander John Heath, Staff Officer (Operations) to ACOS, who was questioned about his duties. He told the Board: 'I have all dealings with ships wishing to enter, or go from, the Scapa anchorage. I therefore have control over the opening and closing of the gates.'

'We take it that you are generally concerned with all the defences at the entrances?' – 'Only in an indirect way, sir, the direct responsibility being with the XDO [Extended Defence Officer].'

'Can you tell us of any officer besides the Admiral who is directly concerned with the general security of the base and the defence of its seven entrances?' – 'There is no one but the Admiral and the XDO and his staff. He has assistant people, I believe, at various entrances.'

'How long has the Chief of Staff been here?' – 'The present Chief of Staff arrived here the day before *Royal Oak* sank. Previous to that, Captain Fellowes performed that duty. The details of the defence were compiled by Captain Fellowes and the Flag Captain. The Flag Captain controlled the drifters and organised the drifter patrols for all the entrances.'

'How long was Captain Fellowes here?' – 'He was here from approximately, I am not certain, August 6 to October 11.'

'What date did the Admiral get here?' – 'Approximately August 26 [note: a handwritten insertion in the evidence file says 'actually Sunday, August 27].'

'There are seven entrances here, most of which have gaps through which a small submarine could certainly pass in daylight at slack water. Is there any comprehensive defence plan recorded on paper which has been passed on by successive officers to the officers now in charge here?' – 'Yes, the Scapa General Defence Scheme, circulated as soon as we arrived. It is typed.'

'Will you please have us provided with a copy?' – 'Yes, sir.'

'Would that contain such information as a list of the gaps where a submarine might enter and details recording the watch on those gaps?' – 'As far as I recollect, no, only full details of the entrances which have boom defences. It was a long screed. I cannot remember exactly.'

'Have you ever seen a statement regarding the width and depth of these gaps at high water spring?' – 'No, sir, but I have made it my business to find out as much as I could of the matter from various sources.'

'From your experience and knowledge, at how many of these gaps would you think it possible for a small submarine to have entered on the night of October 13?' – 'Two, sir, Hoxa Sound and Kirk Sound.'

After further questions about the defences and the currents in various Sounds, Commander Heath was asked: 'Would it not be your duty to advise the Admiral on these matters or at least to assist him in perfecting the defences of these places?' – 'It has never been brought to my notice that I should take particular action with regard to these matters. I will only amplify this by saying we had a small staff to start with and the day-to-day requirements were so multifarious it was not possible to devote attention to matters which were not immediately before one.'

'Have you been called upon to consider your main defence plan?' – 'No, sir.'

The Board then turned to the question of coast watchers and armed guards for the Scapa entrances, and Commander Heath explained: 'The general organisation is under the control of the District Officer of Coastguards, Captain Buchanan, at Wick, the details of which I am not acquainted with.'

'Presumably his watchers cover the whole of the Orkneys?' – 'Yes, sir.'

'Have you ever heard of any coast watchers whose special duty was to observe night and day the five, six or seven passages through which a small submarine might enter?' – 'I know of no such detailed organisation.'

'Do you know if any lookouts are placed on shore at any of these seven entrances that have been mentioned?' – 'Not permanently, sir, that I know of. That was not the case until after October 13.'

'Can you say how the first news of the *Royal Oak* attack reached *Iron Duke* or ACOS?' – 'A signal was received through the PWSS. Flotta, at 0135, I think, on October 14 from *Pegasus:* "General. Send all boats."'

'Would that have been a flashing or wireless signal?' – 'That was a visual, sir. A further signal was received some half-hour later from *Pegasus*: '*Royal Oak* is sinking after several internal explosions.' That is my recollection, sir. The PWSS to *Iron Duke* was telephoned, but from *Pegasus* to PWSS was made by visual.'

'Then the first intimation of enemy attack and sinking of *Royal Oak* was by means of a visual morse signal to PWSS?' – 'Yes, sir.'

'Would this have been much slower than if rockets or Very lights had been fired?' – 'Possibly, sir, but more information was conveyed.'

'When and how was it first made clear to the Admiral that an enemy attack had been made on *Royal Oak*?' – 'The first suggestion that enemy action had been taken was a message from Captain Benn which reached the Admiral within one and a half hours of *Royal Oak* sinking.'

'What action was taken on receipt of the *Pegasus* signal?' – 'Rescue work. All available boats were sent to the scene of the occurrence as soon as possible. The movement of destroyers I cannot give you with any degree of accuracy without further reference. This matter was dealt with by the Chief of Staff.'

Admiral French was now recalled for the last time.

'What date did you arrive here, please?' – 'I was here for five days in June and then I took on my duties on the Sunday before the declaration of war. That is, August 27.'

'Were you given by anyone here a defence plan giving comprehensive details of how the base was defended?' – 'Yes, there was an interim defence plan prepared by Rosyth which was given to me.'

'Was anyone here generally responsible for the defence of the base before you arrived?' – 'The Senior Naval Officer was Commander Frewen and the person who was directly responsible was the Commander-in-Chief, Rosyth.'

'What exactly is the responsibility of the XDO at the present time?' – 'The XDO is responsible for the passage of vessels in and out of the Hoxa and Switha booms, and, in conjunction with the shore batteries, to prevent the passage of enemy vessels. He is not actually responsible for the maintenance of the booms in any way or for the manner in which they have been laid down.'

'There are at Scapa seven entrances, of which three are closed with booms, but each of the booms has a permanent gap at its shore end. When you took up your duties were you satisfied with the state of defence and the lookout arrangements at the seven entrances?' – 'No, my reaction was to ask for more patrol vessels in order that I could have two at each boom with certainty.'

'You told us in your previous evidence that you thought the *Royal Oak* submarine had probably entered through Hoxa boom. Were you more concerned with the safety of the boom entrances and the other four, and, if so, why, please?' – 'Because I thought that following another ship through the gate was much the easiest method of getting into the Flow.'

'Have you had time personally to examine the other four entrances?' – 'I have only examined the Kirk and Skerry Sounds and that was at high water only.'

'Evidence given to us has suggested that there was room for a small submarine to pass in at certainly five of the seven entrances if the conditions were favourable enough. Can you say what defence there was in the shape of shore lookouts on these gaps, guns to cover them, or rapid method of signalling by rocket or Very light?' – 'There were no shore lookouts except at Stanger Head, which covered Hoxa and Switha booms, where there are also guns to cover these booms. At the Hoxa, Switha and Hoy entrances there were the patrol drifters when available. At the four entrances at Holm and Water Sounds there was only an occasional drifter patrol, no lookouts, no guns and no coastwatchers.'

'Did you at any time suggest that more blockships were desirable?' – 'Yes, I was sent up here in June last and one of the things the Commander-in-Chief asked me to look out for was the question of whether more blockships were required. I saw the survey that had been made and went out and personally visited, and passed through, both Kirk and Skerry Sounds. I reported that, in my opinion, there would be no difficulty for a submarine to come in by either of these two Sounds at slack water. It was my opinion that the other two Sounds were impassable to submarines on account of the natural navigational difficulties, assisted by blockships that were placed there. I do, however, consider, now that a German submarine has entered the Flow, that we can no longer rely on the psychological aspect that we had resulting from the last war, and we must make all these entrances absolutely 100 per cent proof.'

'What blockships have been placed between the date of your

report in June and October 13?' – 'One blockship has been placed in Skerry Sound which, in my opinion, completely blocks that Sound. Another blockship has been placed today in Kirk Sound, the *Lake Neuchatel*.'

'Do you consider that the four eastern gaps could be made entirely secure with blockships or would you prefer to have shore lookouts, guns and lights in addition?' – 'I have come to the conclusion that, since we know that a submarine got into the Flow, we must have lookouts, searchlights and guns at all four entrances.'

'Is there in the defence organisation any arrangement for urgent signals to indicate that a ship is in need of immediate help?' – 'None other than are laid down in the signal manual.'

'Will you say what action was taken when you received *Pegasus*'s signals on the night of October 13–14?' – 'I cannot give you times without reference to the signal log, but I immediately ordered all boats and drifters to be sent, made a general signal to raise steam with the utmost despatch and ordered RA(D) [note: Rear-Admiral, Destroyers], through the telephone, to send his destroyers out into the Flow to search for a submarine.'

In the course of the inquiry it emerged that one man who actually claimed to have seen the U-boat had been allowed to return to the Royal Marine Barracks at Portsmouth. He was Marine Owens, Bandmaster, Second Class, who was quite positive about the matter although, in the light of what is known now about the range of Lt. Prien's attacks and his immediate departure after the second of them, it seems fairly certain that Marine Owens was deceived by the upturned gig of *Royal Oak* with one or two men sitting on it. But, at the time, the Board found his evidence impressive.

It came initially in the form of a signal, sent at 1530 on October 21, by the Commandant of the Royal Marine Barracks to Admiral Drax. The signal read: 'Marine Owens, Bandmaster 2nd Class, demonstrably states abandoned ship port side, swam aft accompanied by officer, tall and wearing night clothing. When some 300 yards astern of *Royal Oak*, companion drew his attention to something in water. Owens is emphatic saw clearly conning tower of submarine some 300 yards distant from him, starboard side of *Royal Oak*, submarine appearing to be stationary. Owens unable to trace companion but certain of above facts. Owens later swam to drifter, did not look out for submarine again.'

The Board asked for further details and, on October 23, received a verbatim copy of a report telephoned by the Commandant of the Royal Marine Barracks at 1200 that day. It said: 'I carefully examined Marine Owens on his arrival here from Thurso and obtained the following statement: "I went to the quarter-deck on the second explosion by the officers' ladder and abandoned ship over the port side and got to barnacles and went into water. My one idea was to get clear of the ship. I went over in company with another person, I think an officer. He was wearing pyjamas and was very tall.

' "After we got 300 yards from the ship, we trod water to have a rest. He then said: 'Hello, do you see that over there?' I looked in the direction he pointed and distinctly saw the conning tower of a submarine some 200 (*sic*) yards away. The submarine was on the starboard quarter of the *Royal Oak* and appeared to be stationary. After that I said to my companion we had better make for the drifter, which was lying some 400 yards to the port of the *Royal Oak*. We swam towards the drifter. I then missed my companion and have been unable to trace him since. I am absolutely certain I saw the conning tower of a submarine from my position in the water. I have not the slightest doubt whatever." '

This message ended with the following note: 'The Commandant particularly impressed on Commander Newcombe, Naval Officer in Charge, Thurso, who took in this message that Marine Owens was a first-class witness. He gave his evidence in a simple, straightforward manner without the slightest doubt or hesitation. He was an old soldier of three badges and in every way a splendid character.'

The members of the Board of Inquiry took the testimony of the three-badge Marine, the transcript of evidence, what other facts they had been able to glean, the pile of survivors' statements, surveys of the Scapa defences and newspaper cuttings relating to Lt. Prien's exploit, and retired to consider their findings. But there was no doubt in their own minds now about what had happened.

8

Flowers for a Fallen Hero

The first of two separate reports produced by the Board of Inquiry – one on the entry of a German submarine, the other on the sinking of *Royal Oak* – began uncompromisingly: 'We have obtained no evidence that a submarine was seen or heard entering or leaving the Flow.' Nor, said the Board, had any trace of a submarine been found subsequently. The survivors' evidence suggested, however, that the explosions had been caused by torpedoes fired in one or two salvoes, and the claim by Bandmaster Owens to have seen a submarine was considered accurate.

'We are definitely of opinion therefore that HMS *Royal Oak* was sunk by torpedoes fired from a submarine,' the Board went on. 'Though it is possible that the submarine entered the Flow prior to the night of October 13–14, this is considered unlikely.'

After listing the 11 possible ways a U-boat might have entered the Flow (see Appendix B) and making the point that no lookout was kept at any of the eastern Sounds, the Board continued: 'The weather on the night of October 13–14 was fine and clear and the sea calm. The night was fairly light and for periods the sky was lit up by the Aurora and Northern Lights. High water at Kirk Sound was at 2338 on October 13 . . . Any opinion as to which entrance the submarine came in at must be conjecture only, but in many respects Kirk Sound would present the least difficulty. Having found a way in, the submarine would no doubt aim to return by the same route, but if it entered by Kirk Sound at slack water and left as soon as the torpedoes were fired the tide would then have been *running against it perhaps as much as eight knots*' [note: Board's emphasis].

The Board next went on to say, not without justification, that it considered 'the whole problem of the defences of Scapa required reconsideration' and it recommended a series of measures, most of which Commodore Dönitz, in understandable innocence, had assumed to be already in existence – an adequate force of patrol vessels, asdic defences for boom gates when they were open, minefields, blocking of the eastern entrances, closure as far as possible of the gaps at the sides of booms, lookouts, guns, searchlights, and the extension of boom nets as close to the seabed as was feasible without damaging them.

The whole question of the arrangements for the defence of Scapa Flow that were made prior to the outbreak of war is complex – so complex that a separate sub-committee was appointed to consider the matter before Mr Churchill made his second statement to the Commons about the loss of *Royal Oak* – but the Board now turned its attention to the vulnerability of the eastern Sounds. 'The general feeling at Scapa,' it said, 'was that the eastern entrances to the Flow were considered by the Admiralty to be satisfactorily closed. Local opinion was no doubt influenced by Admiralty message 1546/May 26.'

This message was transmitted after a survey by HMS *Scott*, and it was certainly phrased in confident terms. It said there was 'no, repetition no' risk of a submarine entering Holm Sound (the approach to Kirk, Skerry and East Weddel Sounds) or Water Sound submerged, and entry on the surface would be extremely hazardous and unlikely. Nor would further blocking measures guarantee complete security. It had therefore been decided that 'further expenditure on blockships cannot be justified'.

This confidence seems curiously misplaced, not only in view of what happened but in the light of the contents of the *Scott* report and another submitted at about the same time by Thomas Mackenzie of Metal Industries Ltd. The *Scott* survey estimated the gap between the blockship *Soriano* and the northern shore of Kirk Sound as 820 feet at high water and 500 feet at low water, with 14 feet of water under the bows of the blockship. The Mackenzie figures were 750 feet at high water and 460 feet at low water, with 18 feet of water under the bows of *Soriano*.

The *Scott* survey put the gap between the blockship *Thames* and the southern shore of Kirk Sound as 1,050 feet at high water and 720 feet at low water, adding: 'This channel is obstructed by submerged wreckage [of the blockship *Minich*] . . . but a channel 250 feet wide remains in which a depth of 22 feet could be carried.' The Mackenzie report described the southern gap as 'a 400ft. channel giving 4.5 to 5 fathoms [27–30 feet] at low water between the broken portions of the blockship *Minich* and the two-fathom [12 feet] line on the Lamb Holm [note: southern] shore.'

The Board made the point that the situation was even more hazardous than these figures indicated. At high-water springs, the state of the tide on the night of October 13–14, a U-boat would have another nine feet of water to play with. It also drew attention to what it described as 'two very striking paragraphs' in the Mackenzie report. He had written: 'At the present time a good-sized tramp steamer could enter Skerry Sound without serious difficulty on a course west true, and a similar vessel could, with careful navigation, pass to the south of the block-ships in Kirk Sound. Water Sound and East Weddel Sound could be entered with a vessel such as a 500-ton or 600-ton coaster at high water. Our tug *Imperious*, draught 12ft.6ins., passed in and out of Water Sound recently round the bows of the [blockship] *Naja* at low water.'

Although the Board did not mention it, the Mackenzie report had then gone on to give an absolutely specific warning that, in the event of war, any ship anchored in Scapa Flow might be considered at risk: 'It is fully recognised that the navigation of the Sounds, even now, presents difficulties owing to the strong tidal stream and the existing obstructions, but it is safe to assume that an intrepid submarine officer in wartime would take risks which no discreet mariner would think of taking in peacetime. The possibility of a hostile submarine entering Scapa Flow if the Sounds are left as at present cannot therefore be excluded, and the fact that any such craft successful in passing through one of the Sounds could be within torpedo range of capital ships in 15 to 30 minutes makes it of vital importance that the Sounds should be efficiently blocked.'

The Admiralty decision not to spend money on more block-ships, despite these ominous figures and comments, inspired protests from the Commanding Officer, Coast of Scotland, and from the C.-in-C., Home Fleet, the latter quoting Admiral French's view that he would be happy to take a submarine or destroyer through Kirk or Skerry Sounds 'provided I could see and select slack water to do it in.'

These protests, as mentioned earlier, resulted in the *Cape Ortegal* being placed in Skerry Sound on September 8 and the ordering of the *Lake Neuchatel*, designed to seal off Kirk Sound, which actually arrived the day after *Royal Oak* was lost.

The Board agreed that this confusion about what was needed had not been helpful to the officers who arrived at Scapa Flow a few days before the outbreak of war. It said: 'That [the defences] were not entirely efficient was known, but the extent to which they were vulnerable was certainly not generally appreciated. In the past various officers have been responsible for various sections of the defences, but it appears that no one officer has been responsible for the whole of it. Admiral Commanding, Orkneys and Shetlands, has not got sufficient patrol vessels. There are about 40 drifters under his orders, manned by civilians, but when asked to assist with patrols the crews were not willing to do so. Had they volunteered, or had there been means to compel them to assist, the situation as regards patrol craft would have been very different.'

The Board also agreed that, despite its deficiencies, the Scapa defence scheme had Admiralty sanction, and that ACOS and his staff, nearly all retired officers, had been 'constantly harassed by current administrative work'.

The Board went on to give the positions of *Royal Oak* and *Pegasus*, the only two vessels in the north-east corner of the Flow at the time of the sinking. 'The position of *Royal Oak* on the night of October 13–14, 1939, was 185 degrees, 1.7 miles, from Scapa Pier light. She is now lying with bows approximately 044 degrees. The position of *Pegasus* on the same night was 205 degrees, 9.2 cables (1,840 yards) from Scapa Pier light.' This is not quite accurate. *Royal Oak* was a hundred yards closer to Scapa Pier light and slightly north of west of the position given by the Board. In a letter to me, the Wreck Section of the Hydrographic Department of the Ministry of Defence stated: 'The position given on November 6, 1939, by the King's Harbourmaster at Scapa Flow was: "The stern lies 259°, 4,590ft. from Gaitnip, with the bows 052°, 620ft. from the stern". This gives exact position 058° 55' 50" N, 002° 59' 00" W.'

In one of several appendices, the Board analysed three newspaper cuttings clipped from the *Scotsman*, the *Daily Record* and the *Aberdeen Press and Journal*. They described how Lt. Prien had slipped into Scapa Flow through the defences; one torpedo was fired at *Repulse*, more than half-hidden by *Royal Oak*, but identified by her two funnels; *Repulse* was hit, 'the bows, as we established beyond dispute, sinking deep into the water'; a second torpedo struck *Royal Oak*, which blew up violently. The *Aberdeen Press and Journal* was the only one to contain the story of the car driver on the shore. It was also the only cutting to mention that the attack had been made easier because of the Northern Lights, 'the brightest I have seen in 15 years at sea', Lt. Prien explained.

The Board found a number of points in the cuttings puzzling. It said: 'The reports are interesting and provide a certain amount of information, but not enough to enable us to decide by which entrance the submarine came in. Lt. Prien is careful to speak of "two torpedoes" and never admits that he fired one or two salvoes. The reason for this is not clear. If we assume that most of his statements are intended to be truthful, it appears that he fired first at *Pegasus* beyond *Royal Oak*, thinking that *Pegasus* was the forepart of *Repulse*, covered by *Royal Oak*'s forecastle. His first shot certainly hit *Royal Oak* with one torpedo under the forecastle. All evidence from *Royal Oak* suggests that she was hit later by a salvo of three, but Lt. Prien says: "The effect of the second torpedo was queer. Several columns of water rose high from the ship's sides and columns of fire were visible in all the colours of the rainbow." This matter can only be cleared up by divers, who have not yet completed their examination.

'If it be true that only two torpedoes were fired, we must assume that they came from a specially small submarine with only one or two tubes. Prien remarks on seeing shaded anchor lights, which is correct and authentic. His alleged statement: "As I left port I heard two explosions and saw a column of water rising from the ship furthest north" is obviously untrue. The time between the first and second torpedoes was certainly not less than 10 minutes . . .

'Prien, speaking of the car . . . says: "It stopped and the driver got out, apparently to take a good look at us." He is hardly likely to have invented this. The only place where a car is likely to have been so close to the water is on the road running eastward from St Mary's along the north shore of Kirk Sound. No motorist has made a report so we presume that the submarine was not observed from the car. The exact passage where it entered and left remains a matter of great uncertainty, but Kirk Sound is one of the more probable.'

The Board's second report, which dealt with the sinking, recorded that, when Captain Benn went toward following the first explosion and learned that water was entering the inflammable store, no one thought there had been a torpedo attack. Captain Benn ordered salvage pumps to be started and preparations made for opening and examining damaged compartments. In his own words: 'I had no thought other than that a local explosion had taken place in the inflammable store . . . I felt no uneasiness about the safety of the ship.'

At 0116, 12 minutes after the first explosion, there had been three more shattering explosions, roughly between A and X turrets, accompanied by columns of water. 'The ship at once started to heel to starboard, and, with only a slight hang for perhaps three or four minutes, heeled over with increasing velocity until she capsized about 0129', the Board explained. 'From the moment at which the second [series of] explosion[s] occurred it was practically impossible to do anything effective to save the ship . . .'

An officer and warrant officer, who had gone below to make an inspection, were in No. 3 dynamo room when the second, third and fourth explosions took place. In their opinion, the second explosion had been well forward, the third abreast of the boiler rooms, and the fourth probably at the starboard wing engine room. 'After the fourth explosion,' said the report, 'the forward bulkhead of the dynamo room and the wing engine room began to bulge inwards and steam began to escape . . .

'. . . the Marines' messdeck was swept by flames and full of smoke and fumes. Several hammocks caught fire and were extinguished by men near them. There is also evidence that holes appeared in the decks and that the decks caved in . . . During this period there are several reports of men being blown through doors, up hatches and out of scuttles. By the time the ship capsized a large number of men had reached the water via the forecastle and quarter-deck. It appears that few men were saved from the engine and boiler rooms . . .

'Men who tried to man the launch at the starboard lower boom had a terrifying experience. They could not cast off from the boom and saw the ship turning over on top of them. Metal from the foretop fell into the launch and sank her, and the funnel came down into the water between the launch and the ship's side. One man from the sunken launch was partially sucked into the funnel and then blown out again. Others saw A and B turrets swing round and "fall into the sea." '

This report goes on to say: 'Considering that the ship was in harbour and the sea was calm, the loss of life appears to have been very heavy. We put this down to the fact that the ship was at air defence stations so that an abnormally large number of men were stationed below the main deck. Their escape from the ship was probably impeded by the number of watertight doors that were closed. It has also been stated that a number of men probably took shelter under armour and between decks in the belief that an air raid was taking place . . . In regard to the scuttles and deadlights, we do not consider that closing these would have saved the ship. It might, however, have caused her to sink more slowly and to heel over less violently in the first five or 10 minutes. Had this happened the loss of life would probably have been smaller.'

The separate sub-committee appointed to consider the whole question of the Scapa Flow defences in more detail consisted of the Second and Fourth Sea Lords, assisted by Admiral Drax, and its report made sorry reading. For 21 months the matter of the vulnerability of the eastern Sounds had been under review without being satisfactorily resolved. There had been constant changes of opinion about what channels existed and what ought to be done about them, the whole situation being aggravated by the reluctance of the Admiralty and the government to spend money.

A similar situation existed over patrol craft. ACOS had informed the Admiralty on September 8 that he needed 15 fast craft to patrol booms and indicator nets in his command because drifters were too slow. This request was approved on September 20. But just how ill-prepared Britain was for war is highlighted again by the subcommittee's admission that there had been 'some difficulty in finding and manning suitable craft' with the result that the first four did not leave the Clyde for Scapa Flow until October 25, more than a week after Lt. Prien's exploit.

The sub-committee then proceeded to give its summary of the situation on the night *Royal Oak* was lost. 'Our main comment is on the absence of patrol craft or guns and searchlights at the eastern Sounds. The Admiralty view was that any attempt to enter the Flow by any of the eastern Sounds was extremely unlikely. At the same time it recognised that security was not complete without patrol craft. That the Commander-in-Chief, Home Fleet, shared this view and considered that patrolling the eastern Sounds was necessary was shown by his asking (after the Admiralty decision not to carry out further blocking) for three craft for this purpose, and by his letter of June 28, 1939, in which he said that, if three channels then still considered to be open were to be closed by blockships, patrol vessels would be unnecessary.

'But it was known on the night of October 13 that one at least of these channels remain unblocked. It is true that the Admiral Commanding, Orkneys and Shetlands, had only five drifters* at his disposal at the time, of which one would be boiler cleaning and two were patrolling the booms, but the local orders made no provision for patrolling the eastern Sounds. We conclude that the risk of an enemy submarine entering by the eastern Sounds, which the Admiralty itself had considered to be very slight, was accepted by the Commander-in-Chief, Home Fleet, and the Admiral Commanding, Orkneys and Shetlands.

'As regards blockships, we are left with the impression that the problem of blocking the eastern Sounds before the war was not handled as adequately as its importance deserved . . . On May 26, 1939, as we have observed, the Admiralty decided against buying further blockships. On July 10, in response to representations by the Commander-in-Chief, Home Fleet, the Admiralty modified their decision in respect to the gaps in Kirk Sound and Skerry Sound. Had this decision been taken in May

* The *Pink List* indicates that the number was actually six.

the last ship would no doubt have been sunk in Kirk Sound before October 13 instead of after.

'We do not wish to imply that the Admiralty decision of May was necessarily wrong. The real fault lay in the variety of views of what was required. The report of the Commanding Officer, Coast of Scotland, early in 1939, his second report in March, 1939, and the Commander-in-Chief, Home Fleet, in June, 1939 . . . all gave different estimates of the requirements.'

And so 833 officers and men of the Royal Navy and Royal Marines met their death at a time when they believed themselves safe in an unassailable anchorage. On November 8, Mr Churchill rose to make his second statement in the House of Commons. 'It is now established,' he said, 'that the *Royal Oak* was sunk in the early hours of October 14 by a German U-boat which penetrated the defences of the land-locked anchorage of Scapa Flow . . . Neither the physical obstructions nor the patrolling craft were in that state of strength and efficiency to make the anchorage absolutely proof, as it should have been, against the attack of a U-boat on the surface or half-submerged at high water. Measures had been taken and were being taken to improve the physical obstructions, and the last blockship required reached Scapa Flow only on the day after the disaster had occurred.

'. . . the long and famed immunity which Scapa Flow, with its currents and defences, had gained in the last war, had led to a too-easy evaluation of the dangers which were present. An undue degree of risk was accepted, both at the Admiralty and in the Fleet. At the same time, I must point out that many risks are being accepted inevitably by the Fleet and by the Admiralty as part of the regular routine of keeping the seas, and these risks, which were unadvisedly run at Scapa Flow, seemed to highly-competent persons to be no greater than many others.

'No more striking measure of the strong sense of security against U-boats which covered Scapa Flow can be found than in the fact that, after one torpedo from the first volley had struck the *Royal Oak*, none of the vigilant and experienced officers conceived that it could have been a torpedo. The danger from the air was the first apprehended, and large numbers of the crew took up their air raid stations under the armour, and were thereby doomed, while at the same time the Captain and Admiral were examining the alternative possibilities of an internal explosion. It was in these conditions that the second volley of torpedoes was discharged.'

The report on the loss of the *Royal Oak* had by then begun its circulation around the Admiralty, in the course of which it picked up two annotations from the Director of Naval Ordnance. The first dealt with the possibility of a magazine explosion: 'The report and the evidence indicate that the explosives carried on board did not contribute the loss of HMS *Royal Oak*.' The second was concerned with the vulnerability of the battleship's protective blisters below the waterline. 'The bulge protection of ships of the *Royal Sovereign* class [note: this included *Royal Oak*] was added about 1922,' it said, 'and was estimated to be proof against a torpedo warhead with a charge content of 450 to 500lbs. *Royal Oak* was hit by at least four in number torpedoes. It is believed that the charge carried is as potent as that carried by British 21-inch torpedoes, viz. 750lbs TNT. It is to be expected therefore that the bulge protection would be defeated although there is direct evidence of this only in the case of the torpedo which struck abreast of the starboard wing engine room.'

Only one ritual now remained in order that the incident might be considered closed, at least for the time being – the selection of a scapegoat. The axe fell upon the man who, back in the summer when the world was still at peace, had warned the C.-in-C., Home Fleet, that he would be perfectly willing to take a destroyer, let alone a submarine, through Kirk Sound if the conditions were right. Admiral Sir Wilfred French, ACOS, was placed on the retired list.

'I think they always blame the man on the spot, don't they?'

says his widow, Lady French. 'I was just happy to know that he was going to be home for Christmas.' Placing the blame solely upon Admiral French, however, appears to have been an excessively harsh and unjust decision. It was hardly his fault that the eastern Sounds were not adequately blocked, were not patrolled and were not defended by searchlights and guns. For patrol purposes he had at any given time two Fleet drifters, which were committeed to the booms, thought quite rightly to be, if anything, more vulnerable than the eastern Sounds; the five searchlights in the Orkneys were set in emplacements pointing out to sea in the hope of detecting a seaborne German invasion; and, of the 16 guns on land, five were married to the searchlights as an anti-invasion measure; eight were committed to the defence of the oil fuel depot at Lyness against air attack; and the three Bofors at Netherbutton were to provide the same service for the RDF station.

That blaming Admiral French was a piece of political tidying-up is suggested by the fact that he was shortly afterwards given a supervisory job concerned with British ports, and, from 1941 to 1944, served as British Administrative and Maintenance Representative in Washington. 'When we came home,' says Lady French, 'it was only because of our daughter's schooling. The Admiralty wrote me a very nice letter when my husband died.'

A small contribution towards righting the wrong done to Admiral French is contained in the first volume of *The War At Sea*, the official history of the naval war between 1939 and 1945, by Captain Stephen Roskill, which says: '. . . the First Lord finally reported to his colleagues that the senior officers on the spot had not taken adequate measures to improve the defences of the base. The just allocation of responsibility must always in such cases be difficult, but it does now seem that the true causes went deeper than the conclusion quoted above and that the loss of the *Royal Oak* was the result not so much of a failure by the officers on the spot, who had in fact several times represented the weaknesses for which they were censured and had done their best to remedy them, as the policy of the government of the day and the failure of the Admiralty to obtain proper priority in time of peace for the defences of the Fleet's chosen base.'

In 1941, when Admiral French left for Washington to take up his new post there, *Royal Oak* had already been avenged . . .

In the first week of March, 1941, *U-47* was one of a pack of three U-boats harrying convoy OB293. At 0010 on the night of March 7–8, the 5,258-ton British merchant ship *Dunaff Head*, bound from Glasgow to St John, Newfoundland, was torpedoed some 300 miles off the coast of Iceland. Although it was a misty night with visibility less than a mile, Lt.-Cdr. James Rowland, commanding officer of one of the escort vessels, the destroyer *Wolverine*, did not fire a starshell but simply maintained course and speed.

Twenty-three minutes later, her crew sighted smoke resembling diesel exhaust. Almost simultaneously hydrophone effect was reported on the same bearing. *Wolverine* altered course, increased speed to 18 knots and signalled her companion escort vessel, HMS *Verity*. At 0026 *Wolverine* sighted first a wake, then a U-boat. Lt.-Cdr. Rowland ordered full speed and course was altered to keep bows-on to the U-boat, which was zig-zagging. It had been decided not to fire until close enough for an attack to be decisive. When *Wolverine* was still 1,400 yards from her target, however, *Verity* fired a starshell and the U-boat immediately dived.

For several minutes contact was lost, but at 0038 *Wolverine* picked up another firm echo at a range of 1,300 yards. For the next two hours, the destroyer and the U-boat played cat-and-mouse in the mist and darkness. Finally, at 0359 loud hydrophone effect was picked up again, indicating that the U-boat had surfaced. A quarter of an hour later it was confirmed that a U-boat was the source. *Wolverine* increased speed to 18 knots and the events of the next 90 minutes were later the subject of a dramatic description in one of the Admiralty's *Monthly Anti-Submarine Reports:*

There followed a remarkable chase of the U-boat on the surface . . . for which the greatest credit is due to *Wolverine*. The U-boat was followed at 20 knots with reductions of speed to eight knots every five to 10 minutes in order to regain hydrophone effect. At 0518, while proceeding at 20 knots, *Wolverine* sighted the wake of the U-boat fine on the starboard bow and, one minute later, the U-boat itself. *Wolverine* altered course a few degrees and increased speed to ram, but the enemy dived when she was 200 to 300 yards distant.

Phosphorescence and crystal-clear water enabled the U-boat's position to be judged with considerable accuracy. A rush of bubbles was creating disturbed water out of which ran a V-shaped track about 20 yards in length, tapering finely and curling to starboard. Bubbles could be seen underwater near the point of emission. *Wolverine*'s commanding officer was firmly convinced that the track was caused by air escaping from the bow buoyancy vent. The large patch of disturbed water was thought to be air from the main ballast vents and possibly some phosphorescence around the conning tower.

As *Wolverine*'s bridge passed over the centre of the large patch, the order, 'Fire one and hard a-port', was given. Nine more charges with shallow settings were fired at four-second intervals . . . Great disappointment was felt when wreckage did not appear after this attack.

Briefly, *Wolverine* lost all contact with her target, but echoes were picked up again at 0531. Ten minutes later, the destroyer fired another pattern of depth charges. This attack was followed by what seemed to be a faint orange light, subsequently thought to have been a rescue buoy. Then all contact was lost.

Wolverine did not stop for any protracted investigation, but rejoined the convoy. It later became clear, however, that three U-boats had been involved in a concerted attack on OB293 – *U-47*, which had discovered the convoy in the first place; *U-70* (K/Lt. Joachim Matz), sunk the previous afternoon by HMS *Arbutus*, which picked up 26 survivors, including the commander and three other officers; and *U-99* (K/Lt. Otto Kretschmer), sunk later.

U-47 was never heard from again after the attack by *Wolverine*. There would seem to be no grounds for doubting that Lt. Prien's distinguished and courageous career came to an end in the darkness of that March morning. Yet his death, like his life, has become the subject of dispute. It has been claimed that, although *U-47* was lost, Lt. Prien was not in command at the time, having been arrested for mutiny and either executed, or thrown into a concentration camp, or sent to fight on the Russian front. However, no concrete evidence has ever been produced to support this story.

Lt.-Cdr (now Captain) Rowland, who was awarded the DSO for the destruction of *U-47*, lives today in retirement in Perthshire. During his naval career he served in submarines himself for nearly six years, and from 1932 to 1934 did a commission in *Royal Oak*. On reflection he is convinced that it was his first attack which sank *U-47*.

Over lunch one day he told me: 'Just when I increased to full speed and gave orders to stand by to ram, the U-boat altered course to starboard under full helm and began to dive. I still remember very clearly giving the order: "Starboard 30". I don't think I missed the conning-tower by more than a few feet, perhaps a few inches. The 10 depth charges we fired fell exactly on the spot where the submarine dived. From where I was standing on the bridge it was exactly like throwing something out of the window of a railway carriage and watching it hit the bank.

'I could see the depth charge from the forward starboard thrower describe an arc through the air and fall just where the bows of the U-boat had been. The U-boat was moving forward as the depth charge sank through the water so it must have exploded much nearer the conning-tower.'

At the time, although convinced the attack had been success-ful, Captain Rowland had no means, of course, of knowing the identity of his victim. After seeing OB293 safely on its way, he picked up an inward-bound convoy and returned to Liverpool. During his short spell in port, Mrs. Rowland, who was making her contribution to the war effort by working on the land, presented him with a box of bright yellow primroses, which she had picked herself.

'I put the primroses in a vase in my cabin,' he said. 'Shortly afterwards we sailed again to escort another outward-bound convoy. When we arrived roughly at the spot where I was pretty certain I had sunk a U-boat on the previous trip, I took the primroses out of their vase, went up on deck and scattered them on the sea. It seemed a suitable gesture for one submariner to make to another.'

On his subsequent return to Liverpool, he received a signal from the Admiralty, timed 1334/April 9. It read: 'Their Lordships consider your attack on a submarine on 8th March probably achieved the destruction of a German U-boat. They congratulate you, your officers and ship's company on the skill and perseverance with which both the 20-miles chase and the subsequent attack were carried out. It is possible that the U-boat was *U-47*, commanded by Prien.'

It was not until May 23 that the German High Command announced that Lt. Prien and *U-47* had failed to return from patrol. The brief communiqué ended: 'He and his brave crew will live forever in German hearts.'

9

Things Bad Begun

The controversy which surrounds the loss of *Royal Oak* is nearly as old as the sinking and it is easy to trace the process by which it has persisted and grown.

It was born in two places, 700 miles apart, on the night of Tuesday, October 17, 1939. One was the London office of the *Daily Express* newspaper, the other Thurso, most northerly port on the British mainland. In the *Daily Express* office, Mr Churchill's statement to the House of Commons was already in type when news agency tapes began to tap out a contradictory version of events. It was a translation of a broadcast by Lt. Prien which had been put out simultaneously by every German radio station, and it read: 'It was quite a job to smuggle ourselves into Scapa Flow through all the British defences. Bearing in mind the sinking of the German Fleet there in 1919, I was determined something must be done to avenge them. I saw two British warships to the north of me and discharged two torpedoes at them. I at once turned my boat and left the harbour because I did not want my ship and my crew to be captured. We want to do more work.

As I left port, I heard two explosions and saw a column of water rising from the ship furthest north. This was followed by three columns of fire, one red, one blue and one green. A moment later the other ship exploded. I saw parts of her blown in the air, then the whole ship disappeared. Then I realised the northern ship, too, was seriously damaged. She had two funnels, which proves she was not *Royal Oak*. Just as we were leaving port, intense activity began there. The surface of the sea was lit by British searchlights and several depth charges exploded behind me. And we were fired on, too. You cannot imagine how cheerful and happy I felt when, a few minutes later, a thundering cheer echoed over the sea from my crew.

The text of this broadcast, in tone and content, bears a strong resemblance to the story which was to appear in *Der Angriff*, the newspaper of Dr Goebbels, next day. It contains some inaccuracies which seem pointless (two torpedoes instead of four) and some which were presumably intended for dramatic effect (the reference to depth charges and being fired on). The *Daily Express* was not impressed. The Admiralty denied that any other ship had been damaged in the action. This denial, plus Mr Churchill's statement in the Commons and what little information it had been possible to glean from *Royal Oak* survivors, led the newspaper to begin its story next morning in the following uncompromising terms:

At eleven o'clock last night every German radio station broadcast what they announced as a 'how-I-did-it' talk by the commander of the U-boat which sank the *Royal Oak* at anchor in Scapa Flow. It was a fake. It differed so much from Mr Churchill's official version – in the House of Commons seven hours earlier – and stories by survivors that it was obviously told by someone who knew nothing about it.

The same conclusion had already been arrived at in Thurso by four *Royal Oak* survivors. Twiddling the dial of the radio in the house where they had been billeted following their evacuation from Scapa Flow after the air raid on *Iron Duke*, they picked up an English version of Lt. Prien's broadcast. Naturally enough, they listened to the story he had to tell – and, at the finish, they turned to each other and said: 'The bloody liar.' There had been no twin-funnelled ship near them and most of the broadcast was at such variance with their experience that they concluded, like the *Daily Express*, that it had been made by someone without any personal knowledge of the raid.

One of the four survivors present, Acting PO (as he then was) Tom Blundell, remained convinced that, whoever sank his ship, it was not Lt. Prien. Only when four members of *U-47*'s crew – Wilhelm Spahr, Ernst Dziallas, Kurt Römer and Herbert Herrmann – made the journey to Southsea in 1967 to attend the first *Royal Oak* reunion did he, somewhat reluctantly, change his mind: 'I decided they must have been responsible, otherwise they wouldn't have had the nerve to put in an appearance.'

It is understandable that, from the *Royal Oak* survivors' point of view, a critical climate existed when Lt. Prien's official account of his exploit, his log, eventually appeared in translation in the 1948 edition of *Brassey's Naval Annual*. This was not dispelled by the subsequent publication in Britain of Lt. Prien's autobiography; the memoirs of Admiral Dönitz, indicating that Lt. Prien had positively identified his two victims as *Royal Oak* and *Repulse*; and a spate of books by German writers which perpetuated the legends, many of them false, of that disastrous night for the Royal Navy.

Now that the truth is clear, the problem remains of explaining why, taken in all its aspects, Lt. Prien's story is so frequently at variance with the facts. Certainly the following questions need to be answered:

- Lt. Prien gave an exaggerated account of visibility in Scapa Flow. Why?
- Lt. Prien said he torpedoed a ship which wasn't there. Why?
- Lt. Prien is at some pains to justify his decision to break off the action and escape from Scapa Flow. Why?
- Lt. Prien speaks in his autobiography of destroyers and U-boat chasers flitting about Scapa Flow. This is obviously nonsense, even without knowing the facts. It argues that the Admiralty knew Scapa Flow was vulnerable, but instead of rectifying the situation kept a force of ships with steam up, night after night, to ensure a suitable reception

for the first U-boat commander to take advantage of their generosity. Why did Lt. Prien lend his name to this lie?

- Lt. Prien speaks in his autobiography (as he spoke in his broadcast) of depth charges being dropped as he left Scapa Flow. This again is clearly nonsense: *U-47* was on the surface and the sea was full of men swimming for their lives. In any case, no depth charges were dropped until the following morning. Why did Lt. Prien lend his name to this lie?

- Lt. Prien speaks in his autobiography of being challenged by a destroyer which, 'wonder of wonders', turned aside, despite not having received an answer after asking for a recognition signal. Not only did this incident not occur: to say that it did occur could only make Lt. Prien look a fool. In wartime, destroyers which fail to receive a recognition signal do not obligingly turn aside. They repeat the request with a gun – and if they still do not receive a reply it is time to make one's peace with God. Why did Lt. Prien lend his name to this lie?

- In his log Lt. Prien speaks only of a northern and a nearer ship. Yet, according to Admiral Dönitz, he identified them positively in a radio signal a few hours later as *Royal Oak* and *Repulse*. What happened to make him so positive?

- On his return to Germany, Lt. Prien showed some reluctance about identifying his northern ship. In his broadcast, for example, he said: 'She had two funnels, which proves she was not *Royal Oak*.' In *Der Angriff*, he said the northern ship 'looked like *Repulse*'. Why this reluctance?

The notion that the *Royal Oak* survivors have not, as far as memory allows, told the truth about the night their ship was lost does not stand serious examination. What would they have to gain? At the same time, it is difficult to believe that the man who took a U-boat into the main anchorage of the Home Fleet, sank a battleship and escaped unharmed would lie about it. Apart from the question of character, what would be his motive after the successful accomplishment of a perilous mission?

Yet the German story contains a large number of inaccuracies, as a consequence of which Lt. Prien suffers from a somewhat tarnished reputation outside his own country, and to rewrite it on the assumption that, by and large, Lt. Prien told the truth appears to raise difficulties of credibility. Rewritten, the story would have to read like this . . .

Lt. Prien was cool, courageous and dedicated, a man who did not suffer fools gladly. He had volunteered for a highly dangerous mission; he knew it was considered unlikely that he would return alive; but he was determined to do what he had been sent to do and to bring his U-boat and his crew safely home.

At the crucial stage, things began to go wrong. First, there was the unexpected encounter with the merchant ship off Rose Ness which meant he faced a difficult passage through Kirk Sound with a following tide. No sooner had that been accomplished than Robbie Tullock's taxi appeared out of the night, stopped facing the sea, then drove off rapidly towards Kirkwall.

The reasonable deduction was that the driver had seen the U-boat and driven off to give the alarm. If this were the case, *U-47* could not count on very much time in which to accomplish the mission which had brought her across the North Sea. Nevertheless, Lt. Prien set course across Scapa Flow towards the main Fleet anchorage.

Visibility was about two miles except at odd moments when Northern Lights flickered behind the clouds. Short of the Hoxa boom, which he thought had sophisticated defences, he decided to turn back. There were no targets ahead of him as far as he could see, and, if he continued his course and the car driver raised the alarm, he would have the Hoxa boom between himself and his escape route, Kirk Sound. The chances were that he would then lose both his ship and his crew without accomplishing anything.

U-47 back-tracked, cut across the face of Kirk Sound, found

Royal Oak. From a range of around two miles, it seemed to Lt. Prien that there were two ships, not one. In his running commentary to the crew, Herbert Herrmann recalls, he 'definitely said there were two ships there'. It is an easy-enough mistake to make, particularly on a night which was not spectacularly bright.

In the first attack, three out of four torpedoes disappeared without trace. Lt. Prien again headed for Kirk Sound, but when the Flow – doubtless to his astonishment – remained silent, returned for a second attack. This was followed by sufficient activity to make him feel that Scapa Flow was about to become an extremely unhealthy place for uninvited guests.

One of the uppermost emotions in his mind on regaining the open sea was disappointment at not having achieved more. Another was anger that a dangerous mission had been made even more hazardous, and the whole outcome placed in jeopardy, by a 75 per cent torpedo failure in his first attack.

When he sat down to write his log, he was in no mood to invite cross-examination by gold-braided gentlemen who, having spent the night safely in bed, often suffer from the delusion that they would have done better, had they been at the scene of the action. He therefore took the sensible precaution, like many another hero before and since, of answering a couple of questions before they were asked.

Why had he not attacked the ships in the main Fleet anchorage? There were no ships in the main Fleet anchorage. How could he know that when *U-47* turned back before approaching a point level with the Hoxa boom? It was a very bright night.

That night he sent a radio message that *U-47* was safe, one ship had been sunk, another damaged. By this time the Admiralty had announced the loss of *Royal Oak*. For some reason, those in high places in Germany had come to the conclusion that Lt. Prien's second ship was *Repulse*. Admiral Dönitz therefore put a name to both ships when he wrote his war diary.

Lt. Prien arrived home safely, was told he had torpedoed

Repulse, heard the evidence and didn't like it. Except when cornered by questions, he avoided positive identification of *Repulse* whenever possible. It was not an easy task. His exploit was turned into a propaganda circus, in which he was expected to play his part for the greater glory of the Third Reich. The circus culminated in the publication of a supposed autobiography which was, in fact, largely a fake and could in the long run serve only to make a braggart and a liar of him.

And that, unlikely as it may seem, is precisely what happened.

The book *Mein Weg Nach Scapa Flow* is an extraordinary one. The original German version bears a 1940 date, but it was actually published in Berlin in January, 1941, just two months before Lt. Prien's death, and became a best-seller. By 1952, when the remaining copies were pulped, there were only 140,000 remaining out of a total print of 890,000. Even allowing for the fact that the book had the support of the Nazi regime, a sale of 750,000 copies is a remarkable achievement by a work which, in any contest to find the war memoirs containing the most falsehoods and errors, would start as an odds-on favourite.

Its other remarkable achievement is that it should ever have been taken seriously, particularly by writers versed in these matters. A foreword, dated August, 1940, and ostensibly written by Lt. Prien, contains the assurance: 'In all cases I have adhered to the truth and nearly always I have given to things and persons their proper names . . .' This declaration has obviously carried a good deal of weight.

But the obvious nature of some of the errors in the story of the sinking of *Royal Oak* have already been dealt with, and, if you examine the account in *Mein Weg Nach Scapa Flow* of some of Lt. Prien's other exploits, the situation does not improve. The following is a somewhat condensed version of the sinking of Lt. Prien's first victim, the freighter *Bosnia*, on September 5, 1939. All of the statements underlined are quite definitely either inaccurate or invented.

The *Bosnia* was sighted 'early on the morning' of September 5 as 'the sun rose, blood red'. *U-47* surfaced astern and fired two warning shots. *Bosnia* tried to escape and transmitted an SOS, whereupon *U-47* fired two more shots which struck the freighter, the second setting the cargo of sulphur on fire. The account goes on: 'The crew of the *Bosnia* had been over-hasty in their efforts to escape. One boat had filled with water and was foundering.

'By now the lifeboat of the *Bosnia* had filled with water and the sea had swept over it. A few heads were floating close together, then a wave separated them. In space of a few seconds only a handful were left. A few non-swimmers thrashed about with their arms. Others were swimming with long strokes towards the seaworthy lifeboat of the *Bosnia* . . .'

Mein Weg Nach Scapa Flow goes on to describe the rescue of two members of the *Bosnia*'s crew. The first was a mess-boy, whereupon the following conversation is reported to have taken place:

'Are you the mess-boy?' I asked.

'Yes, sir.'

'Where are you bound for?'

'Glasgow.'

The story then continues: 'He spoke in a Cockney accent . . . a boy from the London slums. "You are trembling. Are you afraid?" He shook his head. "No, I'm only cold, sir." "You will have a spot of brandy later on," I said. He nodded his head and added, perhaps to show his gratitude, "Of course, we got a fright, sir, you can't imagine what it's like; you looks over the water and sees nothing, on'y sky and water, and then suddenly a bloomin' big thing pops up beside yer, blowing like a walrus. I thought I was seein' the Loch Ness monster."'

The Norwegian tanker *Eidanger* had by now appeared on the scene. In addition, *U-47* had rescued a 'skinny' stoker and also taken on board one of the *Bosnia*'s officers who was 'pale, fat and tired'. The 'skinny' stoker was 'painfully thin and his ribs showed up clearly like the bars of a cage. Dittmer grasped him by the arms and began artificial respiration. The First Officer of the *Bosnia* was standing beside me. Looking down at the man he said abruptly, "You Germans are good-hearted people, sir."

'I looked at him standing there, fat, well-fed and probably mighty satisfied with himself. I could not contain myself and said gruffly: "It would have been better if you people had given that poor fellow something to eat in your ship."'

It is easy to detect the hand of the ghostwriter in the clichés of the Cockney accent and the Loch Ness monster, and the hand of the Propaganda Ministry in the clumsy attempt to suggest that the *Bosnia* was a starvation ship, the contemptuous assumption presumably being that nobody in Germany had ever heard of, or guessed at, the existence of the National Union of Seamen.*

It is also interesting to compare the truth with the above account. The *Bosnia*, which belonged to the Cunard Steamship Co., had spent the last week of August loading her cargo of sulphur at Licata in Sicily. The radio was full hourly of rumours of war. Nobody was sure which horse Mussolini would back if hostilities broke out as expected, and, not wishing to anticipate matters, the dock staff at Licata made it as difficult as possible for the *Bosnia* to obtain stores and water and make ready for sea.

---

* The minimum weekly rations of British merchant seamen in 1939 were considerably better than those civilians would have to put up with for the greater part of the war. The scale had been laid down 33 years earlier in a schedule attached to the 1906 Merchant Shipping Act. It provided for water (28 quarts), salt beef (3lb), salt pork (2¼lb), preserved meat (2¼lb), fish (3–4lb), soft bread (3lb), biscuit (4lb), flour (2lb), rice (½lb), oatmeal (½lb), potatoes (6lb), dried or compressed vegetables (½lb), split peas (2–3pt), green peas (⅓pt), onions (3oz), tea (3–4oz), coffee (¼lb), sugar (1¼lb), condensed milk (⅓lb), butter (½lb), suet (¼lb), marmalade or jam (1lb), syrup or molasses (½lb), dried fruits (5oz), pickles (½pt), fine salt (2oz), mustard (¼oz), pepper (½oz) and curry powder (¼oz). The National Union of Seamen had no quarrel with the scale of these rations in 1939, but, in view of the growth of refrigeration, they were pressing for more cold meats, salads and tomatoes to be provided for crews in hot climates.

Finally, Captain Walter Poole, the freighter's Master, sent a raiding party ashore at night to plunder whatever could be found in the agent's store, and, once the party was safely back on board, slipped out of harbour under cover of darkness and set course for Gibraltar. The Declaration of War found the *Bosnia* passing through the Straits. On September 5 she was off the north-west coast of Spain.

Denis Bird,* a 19-year-old cadet, had come off watch at 0800 hours and sat down to the predictable, but satisfying, breakfast that was served every Tuesday morning aboard the *Bosnia* – porridge, followed by steak, onions and sauté potatoes. 'Our ships were known as good-feeding ships all over,' he recalled when I eventually traced him to his present home in Cheltenham. 'Breakfast went to a set routine but was always substantial – curry and rice on Monday, bacon and two eggs on Wednesday, steak, onions and potatoes again on Thursday, boiled fish on Friday, steak, onions and potatoes a third time on Saturday, and bacon and eggs on Sunday.

'There was a joint of the day for the officers' dinner, served at noon each day, and the next day it was heated, covered with hot gravy and served to the rest of the crew. Tea was a fry-up at 6 p.m. Sandwiches of corned beef or cold meat were left out for the night watches and the two-gallon coffee pot was never off the stove, day or night.'

After finishing breakfast, Cadet Bird did some washing, then had his usual shave. He had just undressed and was about to turn in when the ship's siren began to sound the alarm signal of continuous blasts. At 0919 a lookout had spotted the periscope of *U-47* about a quarter of a mile astern. Captain Poole

---

* Cadet Bird was the cocky Cockney cabin boy of *Mein Weg Nach Scapa Flow*. Actually, he lived at 164 Priory Road, Old Green, Birmingham, and was the son of the managing director of a Midlands firm. The skinny, starving stoker was Fireman James Woods of 31B St Andrews Gardens, Liverpool. Fireman Woods was built like a heavyweight boxer, as you would expect of someone whose daily task was to shift several tons of coal.

immediately ordered full speed ahead. A minute later, the U-boat surfaced and fired two warning shots. *Bosnia* responded by transmitting an SOS, whereupon *U-47* fired two more shots, which struck the freighter and set her cargo on fire. Captain Poole promptly gave the order to abandon ship.

'I reached the deck just as the fourth round hit No. 2 and No. 3 hatches,' says Mr Bird. 'I saw a rain of wooden hatch covers and derricks fly everywhere on the foredeck. I made my way to the port boat station. My job was to sit in the stern with the junior apprentice in the bow. It was his duty to let go the forward fall and tend to the painter while mine was to let go the after fall, ship the tiller and steer the boat alongside to pick up the rest of the crew from the rope ladder and lifelines.

'But, since we were on the same side as the condenser water discharge, it was essential that the boat should not be fully lowered until either the discharge had been shut off or the special wooden cover had been lowered to cover it and prevent the boat from being flooded. The Third Mate, who was in charge on the deck, was well aware of the danger and had temporarily made fast the falls when we were just above the discharge. I could see the cover being prepared for lowering.

'At this point, Fireman Woods rushed up out of the stokehold and, either in panic or thinking that we were in shock and did not know what to do, threw the forward fall off the bollards himself. He then jumped over the side, wearing his cork lifebelt. These were made of solid blocks of cork and, if they were not fastened really tightly around the waist, could give you a blow on the back of the head powerful enough to break your neck.* At this time the boat was still going ahead at some five or six knots. When the bow of the lifeboat dropped we began at once to fill up

---

* Fireman James Woods of Liverpool was already dead when picked up by *U-47* and Mr Bird believes this was the cause. In his log, however, Captain Poole suggests that the cause was heart failure resulting from 'immersion in cold water when coming direct from the stokehold'.

from the condenser discharge and the scooping action of the bow under the water.

'Fortunately, the apprentice was very alert. He was able to release the painter and the lower block of the falls which enabled the boat to tow stern first until I could cut the after fall and let us drift clear of the ship. Fireman Woods was then some 150 to 200 yards away from us, quite still, with his face down in the water . . .'

Cadet Bird, who was a strong swimmer, made sure the apprentice was in full control of the situation, then discarded his lifebelt, dived into the sea and swam to Woods's aid. 'I had been supporting him for about half an hour, as far as I could judge, when the U-boat came alongside and picked us up,' he says. 'I was very frightened, very cold and quite tired – Woods was a big fellow, more than 16 stone – and, while his crew began artificial respiration, the Commander gave me a full glass of brandy, saying I could probably do with it. I thanked him for the brandy and for the efforts of his crew to revive Woods. He passed a remark to the effect that we were silly to think we could run away faster than his shell could travel.'

While these events were taking place, the Norwegian tanker *Eidanger* was approaching and Captain Poole was still aboard the *Bosnia*, destroying confidential books by throwing them into the flames. *U-47* proceeded alongside the *Bosnia*'s starboard lifeboat and Lt. Prien ordered the Chief Officer on board the U-boat for questioning. In fact, it was not Chief Officer Richard Turnbull who responded to the command but Second Engineer Tom Bryce, who had changed jackets with the Chief Officer.

'Captain Poole was a Captain, RNR, and "Dickie" Turnbull was a Commander, RNR,' Mr Bird explained. 'Both had had fine reputations as captains of Q-ships' – merchant vessels with concealed armament – 'in the 1914–18 war. They believed they were on a list and, if they were captured and their identity was known, they would be taken back to Germany and executed.

'After a brief conversation, the Commander of the U-boat

ordered the *Bosnia*'s starboard lifeboat to proceed to the *Eidanger*. Just about this time, Captain Poole was seen to dive overboard from the *Bosnia*. The Commander of the U-boat instructed one of the Norwegian tanker's boats, which had appeared on the scene, to pick him up.'

For Captain Poole, once safely aboard the *Eidanger*, there remained the tasks of recording in the last two pages of the *Bosnia*'s log the final moments of his ship's life and the burial at sea of Fireman Woods, the only casualty in the action. The entries read:

*1700/5.9.39. 45°27'N, 9°41'W. s.s. Bosnia torpedoed and sunk by German submarine, sinking in one minute, back breaking amidships and vessel disappearing bow first.** *

And:

1700/5.9.39. 43°39'N, 9°50'W. The Body of J. Woods, fireman, was committed to the sea in the presence of the Master and ship's boy of both ships' companies. Burial service read by myself.

In Lisbon on the following day, all the surviving members of the *Bosnia*'s crew were transferred to the motor vessel *Highland Brigade* for repatriation to Britain. Cadet Bird had barely reached his home in Birmingham when he was summoned to embark on a new career: a telegram arrived, calling him up as a Midshipman, RNR. By an odd coincidence, in view of what was to happen one month later, he reported for duty on September 13, 1939, to *Iron Duke*, headquarters ship of ACOS in Scapa Flow.

In the course of research for this book, my path crossed with David Lees, a former British submariner, who has been engaged

---

* At the time this was written, U-boat logs were still held in Britain and not available for scrutiny, except for *U-47*'s log of the Scapa Flow mission. They have since been returned to the German Military Archives at Freiburg. The log of Lt. Prien's first patrol shows that in all salient respects Cadet Bird's account of the sinking of the *Bosnia* is the correct one.

for four years on a general biography of Lt. Prien. Although in a sense rivals, we frequently cooperated in the face of many difficulties (Mr Lees, whose inquiries were concentrated largely in Germany, found reliable information so scarce in the early stages that he became half convinced that Lt. Prien never existed and was an invention of Dr Goebbels).

Mr Lees agreed that he, too, had been having difficulty with *Mein Weg Nach Scapa Flow* and reported: 'The book omits, as you have probably noticed, the sinking of *Rio Claro* on September 6 and suggests that Lt. Prien's second victim was the *Gartavon* on September 7.

'It describes a voyage to South America by Lt. Prien in a ship called the *Pfalzburg* when he was a merchant navy officer. I haven't been able to trace a ship called the *Pfalzburg*. The book describes a fire aboard the sailing ship *Hamburg* when Lt. Prien was a member of the crew. The fire is not mentioned in the ship's log. The *Hamburg* is supposed to have been wrecked off Dublin in a storm at the end of a voyage from Pensacola. Actually she was wrecked a year later at the end of a voyage from Australia.

'The names of most of the people mentioned in the book, apart from *U-47*'s crew, appear to have been invented. There's also quite a lot of bad language although Lt. Prien did not have the reputation of swearing very much . . .'

Perhaps even more curious in the case of a man who *did* have a reputation for being meticulous is that the name of von Hennig, who had attempted an unsuccessful attack on Scapa Flow in the first World War, appears as 'Kenning' on page 170 of the German edition of the book; and on five occasions, including four times on page 152, the name von Varendorff, one of Lt. Prien's two watch officers, is spelled with only one 'f'. Whatever about other aspects of the book, it hardly seemed likely that Lt. Prien would allow these spelling mistakes to pass him by.

Mein Weg Nach Scapa Flow was published by a Berlin company named Deutscher Verlag, previously, and again now, known as Verlag Ullstein. In the summer of 1978 I wrote pointing out that the book contained a large number of errors and asking if the company could provide any information about how, when and where the book was written: Their reply said:

'The work was written by Paul Weymar . . . In 1940, when the book was first published, the manuscript had been shown to the Oberkommando der Wehrmacht (German High Command) for approval, so there is no doubt that the contents had to be in conformity to the Nazi regime's ideas.

'Correspondence between Paul Weyrnar and the Deutscher Verlag shows that after publication of the work it became clear that some of the facts stated in the book are wrong . . .'

10

*Neger in The Woodpile**

The publication of *Mein Weg Nach Scapa Flow* involved Lt. Prien with a writer and a company whose stories typify in their way a sad period in German history.

Paul Weymar, who died a few years ago, is remembered today as a novelist and the author of an approved biography of Dr Konrad Adenauer, West Germany's post-war Chancellor, but when the Nazis came to power in 1934 he was working on the editorial staff of the quality newspaper *Vossische Zeitung*. His lack of sympathy for the new regime ensured that he was promptly fired and, in addition, banned from the Reichsverband der Deutschen Presse, the journalists' union. Consequently, he was not only out of a job but had no prospect of finding one. It was only through the help of friends, who gave him editorial work in secret, that he was able to support his family.

Verlag Ullstein had been founded in 1877 by Leopold Ullstein, who was cast in the same mould as Harmsworth in Britain and Hearst in the United States, men of vision who took advantage of the mass readership created by compulsory education to build themselves vast publishing empires. He was aided by his five sons – Hans, Louis, Franz, Rudolf and Herman – and by the 1930s Verlag Ullstein was the foremost publishing house in Europe with a highly respected international reputation.

---

* 'A ghost writer, somebody who writes a book for somebody else, is known in German publishing as a Neger, or Negro' – Herr Cyrill Soschka, head of production at the Deutscher Verlag in 1940 when *Mein Weg Nach Scapa Flow* was written, prepared for the presses and published.

It employed 10,000 people, it owned vast printing works, and, in addition to the stream of books which poured from its presses, it published the *Berliner Illustrierte*, Germany's foremost illustrated magazine with a circulation of two million; a wide variety of other weeklies and monthlies; the *Vossische Zeitung*, which had been derelict when Leopold Ullstein rescued it at the turn of the century; the popular daily, the *Berliner Morgenpost*; and the successful evening newspaper *BZ am Mittag*.

In 1934 the founder of the firm and one of his five sons, Louis, were already dead. What happened to the remaining four brothers and to their respected company was described for me by another Leopold Ullstein, grandson of the founder. Mr Ullstein, who has lived in London since fleeing from Germany shortly before the outbreak of war, explained: 'By the 1930s we had become largely a Christian family, but the fact that four brothers of Jewish descent should own a big and powerful publishing company was like a red rag to the Nazis.

'They also disapproved of the family's left-liberal political views, which were reflected in the Ullstein publications. The Party did not dare attack us openly, but various undercover pressures were brought to bear. Advertisers were discouraged from using our pages, and it was made clear to readers that it was more desirable to be seen with rival Nazi publications rather than newspapers and magazines from Ullstein.'

The success of this campaign can be seen most dramatically in the case of the *Berliner Illustrierte*, which suffered a 40 per cent slump in circulation – from two million to 1,200,000 – and began to make a loss instead of its former substantial profits. 'My father, Hans, the eldest son, died in the Spring of 1935 at the age of 76,' Mr Ullstein went on, 'and shortly afterwards my three uncles – Franz, Rudolf and Herman – decided that the only sensible course of action would be to try to sell out to the Nazis and salvage what they could.'

The go-between in the delicate negotiations which followed

was Professor Karl Haushofer, German originator of the specious 'science' of geopolitics. Geopolitics, which purported to explain 'the dependence of a people's domestic and foreign politics on their physical environment', provided, superficially at least, a rational basis for Hitler's ambition to unite all the German people under one Reich, and, similarly, with its *Lebensraum* (living space) theory, a justification for his expansionist plans.

Professor Haushofer, who also coined the slogan *Ein Volk, ein Reich, ein Führer*, was a friend of a brother-in-law of the Ullsteins and, furthermore, of Rudolf Hess, the deputy Führer, whom he had taught in Munich in the 1920s. 'Eventually a deal was worked out whereby the Nazis acquired the company for 12 million Reichsmarks [around £1 million], which was about a fifth of what it was worth,' said Mr Ullstein. 'Unfortunately, the money was tied up in bonds, not immediately disposable, and the family received practically nothing in the end.' His Uncle Franz and Uncle Herman departed for the United States, his Uncle Rudolf to London, and the name Verlag Ullstein disappeared from the publishing scene. In 1937, when the company had already been turned into an official Nazi publishing house whose profits were used to finance Party activities, all traces of its Jewish origin were removed by giving it the new, and more patriotic-sounding, title of Deutscher Verlag.

Early in 1940, Paul Weymar reappeared openly on the literary scene with an assignment from Deutscher Verlag to 'ghost' Lt. Prien's autobiography. It is not clear whether he accepted the task out of hunger, patriotism or lack of any choice in the matter. Says Hanns Arens, who now lives in Munich but was one of Paul Weymar's clandestine supporters in the old Berlin days: 'All I know is that he was no Nazi in his personal outlook' – and certainly his decision to co-operate in the writing of *Mein Weg Nach Scapa Flow* was one he lived to regret.

A three-sided contract between Lt. Prien, Paul Weymar and the Deutscher Verlag was signed on February 29, 1940, with each of the signatories receiving an equal share of future royalties. In addition, Lt. Prien was to be paid an advance of 3,000 Reichsmarks (about £150), whose receipt he acknowledged in a letter dated March 4 from his home at 12 Knivsberg, Kiel.

Dear Mr. Weaver ,

There is no need for you at all to apologize for making your request, after all, it is also in my interest that a wrong concep-
tion of the character and personality of my dead husband is
neither created nor let to continue. For that reason I will
glady contribute to clearing up this matter, as is also your
wish.

I will not dwell in detail on the „ inaccuracies" you mentioned, there is also much which I cannot judge objectively.
I can however confirm that my husband had not been able to
correct the final manuscript of his book prior to its going to
print. About a week before the discussions with Mr. Paul Weymar
my husband was called away on business and his book completed
by Mr.Weymar.

It is obvious that the strictly historical course of events
had not been the major concern of Mr. Weymar -- e.g., he
misrepresented my getting acquainted with Günther Prien --
bringing out a exciting book for boys, written in the spirit of
the times, had been most important to him.

For a characterization of my husband's way of thinking I find
Mr. Weymar's words very apt by which he literally quoted
Günther Prien in his letter of protest to the „ Ullstein-Verlag"
-- that is really how he had thought.

Perhaps one chould also take into consideration that this book
appeared at a time at which the German population had entered
into the war and some of the normally valid standards had been
distorted.

Prien's widow, now Inge Sturm, confirms how little opportunity he had to write his own account of the attack.

Some – but by no means all – of the flaws in *Mein Weg Nach Scapa Flow* must have arisen as a result of the speed with which the book was written. The contract called for Paul Weymar to deliver the manuscript by April 15, which gave him only six weeks to obtain his raw material and turn it into an autobiography. During this period, Lt. Prien was available to be interviewed for little more than a week. *U-47* sailed from Wilhelmshaven on March 11, returned on March 29, sailed again four days later, on April 2, and arrived back in Kiel on April 26.

There appears to be no evidence to indicate exactly when Paul Weymar completed his manuscript, but it was some time in the summer of 1940. After making alterations to the account of the Scapa Flow mission, the German High Command returned one copy, officially approved, to Deutscher Verlag on August 23. A second copy, approved by the Propaganda Ministry, was despatched to the publishers on August 27.

U-47 had up to this point had a fairly quiet summer. Apart from one patrol, which lasted from June 4 until July 7, she lay at Kiel, and during these weeks in port Lt. Prien also received a copy of the manuscript. He put to sea out of Kiel again on August 26 and returned to a new base, Lorient on the west coast of France, on September 25. *U-47* carried out two more patrols (October 14–October 23, November 3–December 6) from Lorient before the year was out. It appears that Lt. Prien did not set foot in Germany between his departure from Kiel on August 26 and the second half of December.*

But I did not know any of this background in the summer of

---

* David Lees, who rarely fails to astonish me, says: 'According to the French Maquis agent responsible for the surveillance of U-boat commanders in Lorient Dockyard in 1940, Lt. Prien did not return to Germany until he went home on Christmas leave. At one time he had more than enough to drink on successive nights in port. It was thought he might be cracking up under the strain of too much time at sea, but he appeared to pull himself together.'

1978 when I asked Verlag Ullstein if I might see the file on *Mein Weg Nach Scapa Flow*.

The brothers Franz and Rudolf Ullstein returned to Berlin at the beginning of the 1950s and worked with a number of faithful former employees, including Herr Cyrill Soschka, head of production in 1940, to try to restore Verlag Ullstein to some semblance of its former greatness. The task proved impossible and they sold out eventually to the mammoth Axel Springer organisation.

The Axel Springer headquarters today are in a modern block which towers over the Berlin Wall, close to the celebrated Checkpoint Charlie. A couple of hundred yards away, out of respect for the firm's past eminence and achievements, the name of Verlag Ullstein is preserved on a smaller building, still surrounded by the weed–covered scars of Berlin's wartime devastation.

The correspondence which made it obvious that some of the facts stated in *Mein Weg Nach Scapa Flow* are 'wrong' proved to be an extremely unhappy letter of protest from Paul Weymar, dated June 4, 1955, shortly after he had learned that the book penned by him 15 years earlier was being published, unaltered, in an English edition. His protest, which is a remarkable rejection by an author of his own work, can best be allowed to speak for itself.

News of the English edition, he wrote, had come as 'an extremely disagreeable surprise' and his letter went on: 'In my view a new edition of such books can be justified only when they are placed firmly on the basis of historical truth . . .

'In Prien's case, one is duty-bound in my opinion to correct demonstrably false facts – the account of the Scapa Flow mission was "touched up" in 1940 on understandable military grounds – and also to clarify those other aspects of the war at sea which are given insufficient expression, to say the least, by the juvenile and aggressive style of this book for boys, the hardships and horrors of the U-boat war, which Prien also discovered but was unable to voice at that time.

'I recall one statement which he made to me in confidence: "When I saw the first burning tanker in front of me and thought of the wretched hundreds of men perishing in this dome of flames, I felt like a murderer before the scene of his crime." It should be an obligation to include this and similar utterances in a new edition, also from the point of view of Prien's memory.'

Paul Weymar then made the point that he looked back on his 'co-operation in a type of war literature, the manner in which they presented Prien in the original version of the book, with heavy feelings of guilt. For through such a one-sided representation of real events, romantic illusions about the nature of war are given support and young people are put into an adventurous mood which can only lead to a monumental hangover. I should not like to lay the same guilt upon my shoulders today for the second time . . .

'In the meantime, the three copies of the English edition promised in your letter have come to hand. I was, without exaggeration, horrified. On the back of the book, a swastika, and on the wrapper the announcement that more than 750,000 copies of this book have been sold in Germany. No intimation that this figure was achieved entirely in the Nazi time and through suitable political support, and that the book cannot therefore be regarded as a true publishing success.

'Instead, it goes without saying that the impression will be created that this immense sale was achieved in present-day Germany. I believe one does not have to be versed in politics to foresee what consequences this unscrupulous sales trick will have. Abroad everyone will say: "Look, that's how the Germans are, Nazis today just as they always were." I should not like to be involved in a transaction with such a basis.

'The question which I should like to direct to you runs as follows: "Do you see a possibility of cancelling the deal with The Gray's Inn Press? Or, if the first copies of the book are already on

the market, at least prevent the publication of further copies?"
Should you refuse, I must reserve to myself all further steps on
the grounds set out above. In any case, I should like you to know
right now that I refuse to be involved in any business dealings
relating to the Prien book in its original form and intend to make a
gift of any royalties to charity, should I fail to prevent further
publication of the book here and abroad in its present form.

'As my collaboration in the Prien book has become widely
known, I feel it is necessary, for the sake of my reputation as a
writer, to detach myself publicly from such new editions . . .'

Herr Soschka, now retired, lives in a flat in the suburbs of
West Berlin. Despite three hours of conversation, lubricated
with a bottle of *Schnapps*, he was unable to add much to the
background of *Mein Weg Nach Scapa Flow*.

'In those days, of course, you could publish only what you
were allowed to publish,' he said. 'I simply handled the production. None of the editorial people involved are alive now.' Herr
Soschka met Lt. Prien once: 'It was about Christmas, 1940,
when he was on leave in Berlin. I liked him. He seemed very
cheerful and signed a copy of the book for me.'

Herr Soschka thought it improbable that *Mein Weg Nach
Scapa Flow* could have been published without Lt. Prien's
approval of the text. On the other hand it was difficult to
believe that the man who volunteered for the mission to Scapa
Flow . . . the man who gave a drink to Cadet Bird because he
was cold and showed concern about the men he was forced to
send to their deaths . . . the man of whom Herbert Herrmann
says: 'He hated all the fuss when he was ashore and was always
glad to get back to sea' . . . would willingly lend his name to this
tissue of lies, errors, distortions and jingoistic nonsense.

The one person most likely to know the truth seemed to be
Frau Ingeborg Sturm-Prien, his widow.

Frau Sturm is a jolly and attractive blonde who lives today in
Cologne. According to *Mein Weg Nach Scapa Flow*, Lt. Prien
first saw her as a stranger, a pretty girl standing in a garden,

presented her with a bunch of flowers, later came upon her likeness by accident in a photograph, met her, wooed her and married her. 'Actually,' she told me, 'we first met when we were paired off as table companions at a wedding.'

Her present husband, Herr Paul-Heinz Sturm, a banker turned soldier, was a rival for her hand at the time. They married a couple of years after the announcement of Lt. Prien's death in the spring of 1941. The weeks prior to the formal announcement were traumatic for her. 'Three U-boat commanders, all well known, were lost within a few days of each other,' she said. 'I was informed that *U-47* was missing, presumed lost, but ordered to keep the information to myself. It was thought that the news would be too much of a shock for Germany. For weeks my friends asked: "When is your husband coming home again?" and I had to pretend that he would be.'

She, too, went to Berlin when Lt. Prien and his crew were flown there after Scapa Flow. At the time she made a note, still in her possession, to the effect that her husband was critical of the circus made out of his whole exploit: 'He resented being caught up in the political-propaganda machine. He saw his deed solely as a sailor's achievement.'

'He hated fuss,' she went on. 'After Berlin, we went on holiday to Austria and I remember how uncomfortable he was in the train when people kept nudging each other and pointing him out.' If there was one word to describe him, she would choose the word 'realist'. 'He asked a lot of himself and a lot of others,' she said. 'I know he was disappointed not to have achieved more in Scapa Flow – he told me so – and he was angry about the recurrent torpedo failures. After the Norwegian campaign he visited Berlin and complained forcefully about the whole matter.

'But he always remained a realist and never set himself goals which were impossible to achieve . . .'

Frau Sturm remembers that he received a manuscript of *Mein Weg Nach Scapa Flow*. 'He was very angry and kept crossing things out,' she said. She is quite certain in her own mind, however, that these changes were never made and that he did not know this until the book was published. 'The wrong spelling of the names von Hennig and Varendorff are certainly something he would have noticed and corrected,' she explained.

It would perhaps be neither unfair nor unreasonable to suggest that it was his sense of realism which persuaded Lt. Prien not to press on beyond the Hoxa boom, once convinced that he had been seen by the driver of the car on the shore, and to forestall any subsequent argument about whether his decision had been the correct one.

The suggestion in the war diary of Admiral Dönitz that the appearance of two aircraft over Scapa Flow caused a mass exodus of ships of the Home Fleet and robbed *U-47* of even greater success than was actually achieved indicates a complete German misreading of the situation. This is borne out by other documents in the Military Archives at Freiburg.

The *Luftwaffe Situation Report* for October 13, for example, contains the confident assertion that the reconnaissance carried out the previous afternoon over Scapa Flow showed the presence of seven battleships, 10 cruisers and an aircraft carrier, *Furious*. The report even names the battleships: *Nelson, Rodney, Resolution, Royal Oak, Royal Sovereign, Hood* and *Repulse*. Of these vessels, as has already been made clear, only *Royal Oak* and *Repulse* were in Scapa Flow at the time: *Nelson, Rodney* and *Hood* were at Loch Ewe, *Royal Sovereign* was at Plymouth, and *Resolution* did not belong to the home Fleet.

Similarly, the naval *North Sea Situation Report* on the morning of October 14, a few hours after the sinking of *Royal Oak*, contains the observation that, according to the listening service, 'the battle-cruiser *Repulse* returned to Scapa in the night of October 12–13'. This is a complete reversal of the facts: on the night of October 12–13 *Repulse* proceeded from Scapa Flow to Rosyth.

Finally, on October 15, the naval War Diary noted: 'The damage inflicted on *Repulse* is confirmed by the fact, established by air reconnaissance, that the battlecruiser is lying in dock at Rosyth. An air attack on *Repulse* has been requested.'

The first signals which passed between *U-47* and Germany after the Scapa Flow mission are not in the Freiburg files. In addition, Admiral Dönitz chose not to reply when I wrote to him, raising a number of queries about the exploit. However, David Lees subsequently inquired into the matter of the signals on my behalf by letter. In his reply, Admiral Dönitz stated that he had been informed by telephone that Lt. Prien had made a signal saying he was safe. In the normal manner, he had identified the ship he had sunk as a battleship 'of the *Royal Sovereign* class'.

Mr Lees returned to this topic during a personal visit to Admiral Dönitz, in 1978. Admiral Dönitz he says, repeated that Lt. Prien had referred to his victim as a battleship 'of the *Royal Sovereign* class' and added that the signals from *U-47* had not put a name to the second, or northern, ship. Kapitän-zur-See Hans Meckel, who was the Admiral's Chief of Communications in 1939, was present at this interview. His recollection of the content of the signals was the same as that of Admiral Dönitz and he added that the other messages which passed between *U-47* and Germany were concerned with arrangements to fly Lt. Prien and his crew to Berlin for their audience with the Führer.

Who then had provided the positive identification of *Repulse*? In answer to the direct question, Admiral Dönitz replied: 'The German High Command.'

It need not occasion any surprise that Admiral Dönitz did not argue the point with his superiors. Nor is it strange that Lt. Prien showed reluctance on his return to Germany to accept *Repulse* as his 'northern' ship. He would have been well aware that it was impossible for divers to have examined the damage, for emergency repairs to be carried out, and for the vessel to sail, or be towed, the 250 miles from Scapa Flow to Rosyth in the space of about 40 hours.

The grey ships have long been gone from Scapa Flow to be replaced by the vessels of the oil industry. The wreck of *Royal Oak* lies in less than a hundred feet of water, and, on a calm day, her dark shape can be seen by passengers making the 12-minute journey by air from Wick to Kirkwall. Oil still seeps to the surface from her fuel tanks. The hull, which has now been declared a war grave, is covered with barnacles and the seaweed known as dead men's fingers. The large green buoy which rides the waves above reads: 'This marks the wreck of HMS *Royal Oak* and the grave of her crew. Respect their resting place. Unauthorised diving prohibited.'

Of the 424 officers and men who escaped to fight another day – and, in some instances, to die in the process – about 60 are still alive. They gather in Portsmouth, the depot of their old ship, each October. On the Friday night they meet in a naval club, consume a great deal of beer and rum, and talk about a time when the world was younger and they were at war. Herbert Herrmann comes down from Scotland with his wife each year, and, at the simple service next morning at the war memorial on Southsea Common, lays a wreath. He does not look quite himself because of all the drinks pressed upon him the night before.

'Taffy' Davies organises the reunion. A couple of days before the first one I attended, he telephoned with what he said was an important message. 'I've been telling some of the troops that you're trying to find out what really happened on the night the old gal was sunk,' he explained, 'and they asked me to have a word with you. I know it isn't necessary, but they insisted. They said they hoped you wouldn't be nasty to Herbert or embarrass him in any way.

'He's a very good friend of ours.'

Sources

The following Admiralty and War Office documents, available at the Public Record Office, are those I have relied on for the facts about the sinking of HMS *Royal Oak* and other aspects of the career of Kapitänleutnant Günther Prien from a British point of view:

ADM1/9777   Submarine Intelligence Summaries.
ADM1/9792   Naval Intelligence In Wartime.
ADM1/13721   Summary Of Information On German
             U-Boats, 1943.
ADM1/17561   Report on Captain Gilbert Roberts's Visit To
             Kiel, May, 1945.
ADM1/17602   Particulars Of Enemy Torpedoes, 1945.
ADM16/4205   *The German Submarine Campaign*, by Captain
             (S) Ernest Thring.
ADM136/13   Ship's Book of HMS *Hood*.
ADM182/126   Confidential Admiralty Fleet Orders, 1939.
ADM187/2-4   Pink Lists (showing the whereabouts of HM
             ships at 1600 hours each day) for October,
             November and December, 1939.
ADM189/60   Annual Report Of Torpedo School, 1940.
ADM199/1   Introduction Of Convoy System: Regulations
             And Procedures.
ADM199/130   Anti-U-Boat Attacks, 1939–40.
ADM199/137   Anti-U Boat Attacks, 1939–40.
ADM199/158   Loss of HMS *Royal Oak:* Board Of Inquiry.
ADM199/390   Northern Patrol War Diaries, 1939–40.

ADM199/393   War Despatches of C.-in-C., Home Fleet, 1939–41.

ADM199/1788   U-Boat Incident Signals, 1939.

ADM199/1789   U-Boats Sunk Or Damaged.

ADM199/1895   Lyness Base Records: Scapa Moorings.

ADM199/1939   Daily Operations Report For First Lord.

ADM199/1957   Daily Summary Of Naval Events, 1939.

ADM199/1982   Daily Summary Of Naval Events, January–March, 1941.

ADM199/2032   U-Boat Incidents, September–October, 1939.

ADM199/2033   U-Boat Incidents, November–December, 1939.

ADM199/2057   Monthly Anti-Submarine Reports, 1939–40.

ADM199/2058   Monthly Anti-Submarine Reports, 1941.

ADM199/2130   Survivors' Reports, Merchant Vessels, September–November, 1939.

ADM199/2196   Summaries of Naval War Diaries, October, 1939.

ADM199/2197   Summaries Of Naval War Diaries, November, 1939.

ADM53/   Logs of HM Ships. October, 1939: *Ashanti* (107549), *Aurora* (107577), *Bandit* (107595), *Belfast* (107730), *Bittern* (107781), *Boadicea* (107800), *Bramble* (107828), *Broke* (107889), *Calypso* (107938), *Cardiff* (107693), *Caledon*, (107931), *Colombo* (108072), *Cossack* (108123), *Curlew* (108170), *Delhi* (108256), *Dunedin* (108416), *Enchantress* (108513), *Eskimo* (108564), *Fame* (108642), *Fearless* (108668), *Firedrake* (108690), *Fleet-wood* (108705), *Foresight* (108726), *Foxhound* (108784), *Furious* (108819), *Glasgow* (108895), *Greenwich* (108995), *Guardian* (109042), *Hastings* (109091), *Hazard* (109126), *Hebe* (109138), *Hood* (109200), *Iron Duke* (109327), *Jackal* (109356), *Janus* (109369), *Jervis* (109405),

Jupiter (109418), *Maori* (109718), *Mashona* (109728), *Matabele* (109749), *Mohawk* (109786), *Newcastle* (109922), *Pegasus* (110029), *Pelican* (110039), *Punjabi* (110129), *Renown* (110180), *Repulse* (110192), *St Martin* (110356), *Scotstoun* (110482), *Seagull* (110518), *Sharpshooter* (110544), *Somali* (110652), *Southampton* (110664), *Speedy* (110677), *Stork* (110695), *Sturday* (110706), *Tartar* (110780), *Valorous* (110901), *Wanderer* (111081), *Weston* (111147), *Whitehall* (111158), *Whitley* (111170), *Witch* (111224), *Woolston* (111248). November, 1939: *Devonshire* (108303), *Norfolk* (109959), *Suffolk* (110718).

WO166/114   Scottish Command War Diary.
WO166/1234   Orkney And Shetlands HQ War Diary.
WO166/2049   Orkney Fixed Defences, RA, War Diary.
WO166/2055   Orkney and Shetland Defences, AQ Branch, War Diary.
WO166/2507   226th Heavy A/A Battery, RA, War Diary.
WO166/3551   Orkney Fortress Company, RE, War Diary.
1906 Merchant Shipping Act and attached victualling schedule.
Log of the *Bosnia* (Dept. of Trade).
Log of the *Gartavon* (Dept. of Trade).

In addition, the following published sources were consulted:

Jay W. Baird, *The Mystical World Of Nazi War Propaganda, 1939–45* (University Of Minnesota Press, 1974).
Cajus Bekker, *Luftwaffe War Diaries* (Macdonald, 1967).
Jochen Brennecke, *The Hunters And The Hunted* (Burke Publishing Co., 1958).
Malcolm Brown and Patricia Meehan, *Scapa Flow* (Allen Lane, The Penguin Press, 1968).
Winston Churchill, *The Gathering Storm* (Cassell, 1948).

Grand Admiral Karl Dönitz, *Memoirs* (Weidenfeld and Nicolson, 1959).

Wolfgang Frank, *Enemy Submarine* (William Kimber, 1954) and *The Sea Wolves* (Weidenfeld and Nicolson, 1955).

Alexandre Korganoff, *The Phantom Of Scapa Flow* (Ian Allen, 1974).

Ernst Kris and Hans Speier, *German Radio Propaganda* (Oxford University Press, 1944).

Alexander McKee, *Black Saturday* (Souvenir Press, 1959).

Günther Prien, *I Sank The Royal Oak* (Gray's Inn Press, 1954).

Captain Stephen Roskill, DSC, RN, *The War At Sea, Vol.1* (HMSO, 1954).

William Shirer, *Berlin Diary* (Hamish Hamilton, 1941).

Technical Reproduction Branch, Admiralty, *Führer Conferences On Naval Affairs – Minutes Of Staff Meetings Between Hitler And Various Commanders* (1947).

The Seaman, May 11, 1938.

Daily Express, October 18, 1939.

DerAngriff, October 18, 1939.

The Orcadian, October, 1939.

The following German official sources were also studied at the Military Archives in Freiburg:

RM7/5	*Kriegstagebuch der Seekriegsleitung.*
RM7/266	*Lageberichte Ostsee, Nordsee, Atlantik.*
RM7/279	*Lage Nordsee.*
RM7/329	*Lageberichte West, Luftwaffenführungsstab.*
RM87/2	*Kriegstagebuch, Grossadmiral Karl Dönitz.*

and the logs of *U-47*.

Appendix A

Acknowledgements

In the course of research for this book I have frequently been asked how I became interested in the *Royal Oak* story and set about trying to discover the truth. A brief account may therefore be of interest to some readers and will certainly provide an opportunity of thanking the many people who helped with the task.

Early in 1975 I was asked to write a 3,000-word article about the sinking of *Royal Oak*. It soon became clear that this was impossible because the facts were obscure and there was hardly any aspect of the exploit over which everyone was in agreement. At that time it also seemed that nobody was aware that the Admiralty documents relating to the case had become available with the reduction of the secrecy embargo from 50 to 30 years and anybody with a Public Record Office reader's ticket could consult them.

Mr Frederick Lambert, then in charge of the Rolls Room at Chancery Lane where the indices of Admiralty files were kept at that time, and his staff could not have been more helpful in recommending sources as well as producing them. The same is true of Mr George Donovan and his staff at Ashridge in Buckinghamshire, storage place of the logs of HM ships.

Transcripts of Crown-copyright records in the Public Record Office appear by permission of the Controller of HM Stationery Office.

Mr George Clout and Mr Terry Charman at the Imperial War Museum were equally co-operative in producing books about Lt. Prien in a variety of languages, plus German newspapers of the time, and they also kindly suggested some sources which might otherwise have escaped me.

Mr Herrmann received me courteously in his home on two occasions. Our discussions were hampered to some extent by two factors: he felt he had a prior commitment to helping the author of *The Royal Oak Disaster* – which was, by then, well on its way to the bookstalls – and, I think, he also felt, incorrectly, that I was basically hostile to Lt. Prien's case.

He said at one point: 'Anyone with common sense would know that we were not expected to sink the entire Fleet. The idea was to penetrate the anchorage, do some damage, and get out again. That's what the skipper did – and it makes a man liked by any crew under any circumstances.' I have therefore tried not to involve him in any matters which might be considered contentious.

Between these two visits I flew to Kirkwall and, by pure coincidence, booked into the Royal, the hotel from which Robbie Tullock picked up his passengers shortly before midnight on the night of October 13–14, 1939. The choice was dictated simply by the fact that the Royal was the first hotel I came across with a bar which had a direct entrance to the street. Barmen are always useful allies for strangers seeking information: they meet a lot of people in the course of a day, particularly in the Orkneys where the indications are that nobody has yet died of thirst.

The loss of *Royal Oak* is not a matter of dusty history in Kirkwall. Shops keep a stock of books on the subject; summer visitors hire boats and make a pilgrimage to the site of the wreck; and if you come across a group of men engaged in deep discussion it is an even chance that they are arguing about whether or not Lt. Prien ever saw the inside of Scapa Flow.

Inside 800-year-old St Magnus Cathedral, a plaque commemorates the disaster. It reads: 'In memory of the 833 officers and men of HMS *Royal Oak* who lost their lives when their ship was sunk in Scapa Bay by *U-47* on the 14th October, 1939.' I went to take a look at it before making my way down to St Mary's after lunch. Beneath the plaque lay two wreaths, one from the Kirkwall branch of the British Legion, the other anonymous with the simple message: 'To old shipmates. We remember.'

At St Mary's, I walked through the village, along the coastal road and out onto the Churchill Barrier which was built before the war ended to seal off Kirk Sound and the other eastern entrances. I took some photographs and, back in the village, asked a passer-by if it was possible to make one's way along the top of the cliffs to a point opposite where *Royal Oak* lay. 'It's heavy going because of the thick heather,' he said. 'You'd be better taking the road and cutting across the fields just before you come to the old Radar station. Funny you should mention the *Royal Oak*. We were just having an argument down at the garage about what really happened to her. If you're interested, the man to see is Ronnie Aim at the post office. It's early closing day, but he'll be there.'

It was good advice. Ronnie Aim's family have lived on the shores of Kirk Sound for most of this century and he has been a dedicated Prien-watcher since 1939. 'I was down at Scapa Pier at around 10.30 on the Friday night,' he told me. 'I could see the silhouette of *Royal Oak* quite distinctly. It was a shock next morning to hear that she'd gone. I couldn't believe it.' On this and a subsequent visit of mine, Mr Aim was generous with his time and conversation; provided meals and cups of tea; drove me around in his Volkswagen van; produced Warden Flett and the brothers Park; made a number of valuable inquiries on my behalf; and pointed the way to the driver of the car on the shore.

That particular stroke of good fortune began when I asked if the telephone kiosk outside the post office had been there in 1939 because it would seem more logical for a car driver, if he had seen a U-boat, to look for a telephone rather than drive off into the night. 'There was certainly a public telephone here in 1939,' said Mr Aim, 'but I think it was inside the post office.*

'But about the car. Around here they say that, if there was a car, it didn't come from Kirkwall and turn around and drive back again when it reached the coast road. It came down the incline at the side of the post office and stopped before turning into the coast road. The building at the top is now a Community Centre, but it was a Drill Hall in 1939 and there would almost certainly have been a dance there on a Friday night at the start of the war.' The next morning I checked the files of the local newspaper, *The Orcadian*, but could find no advertisement for a dance and no report of a dance having taken place.

In the afternoon I went to see Bill Sabistan, who commanded the last Royal Navy vessel in Scapa Flow, the Fleet tender *Loyal Proctor*, used for RNR training and for ceremonial occasions. I had been fortunate enough to receive an introduction to him from a friend, Derek Hall, who uses one of his boats when he goes fishing in the Orkneys each year.

After making a telephone call, Mr Sabistan's advice was: 'If you want to know about the *Royal Oak*, go and see David Gorn, the outfitter.' That proved later to be the consensus of the clientele in the Royal Hotel bar.

David Gorn, whose hobby is scuba diving, has the remains – still in good condition, still joined together – of the propeller, gears and electric motor of G7e torpedo no. 2874. He discovered them beside the wreck of *Royal Oak* on Sunday, May 20, 1973. 'I just noticed a gleam,' he said, 'and as soon as I began to scrape the sand away I realised what I had found.' It took two more Sundays to excavate his discovery completely and haul it to the surface on the end of a rope. A week later, his friend Eric Kemp, who has a Kirkwall sports shop, found similar remains of another torpedo, no. 2597, buried near the midships section of the wreck. The gears of both torpedoes, having been cleaned

---

* The postal authorities in Kirkwall were unable to clarify this point.

up, still function perfectly. 'But,' said Mr Gorn, 'the chromium plating on the propellers was in much better shape after 33 years on the seabed than it is now after being exposed to fresh air.'

He has a simple explanation for the failure of naval divers to find the torpedo parts in 1939: 'In those days they clumped around on the seabed in heavy boots and made the water murky.' Mr Gorn and his friend, who had been granted permission to dive in the vicinity of *Royal Oak* providing that they did not take any underwater photographs, enter the wreck or remove anything from it, took the precaution of having their discoveries authenticated. They sent the German Embassy in London a detailed description, plus photographs and the information that one of the propellers bore the inscription 'BMAG/VLS'. As a result they received the following letter, dated July 20, 1973, from Rear-Admiral Werner Schunemann, the naval attache:

Following examinations by German torpedo experts I am now in a position to furnish you with the information required in your letter of June, 1973. Dr Mayer [note: one of the experts] confirms that the fragments are in all probability stern pieces of German torpedoes, type G7e. It is most likely that they are torpedoes fired against HMS *Royal Oak* by submarine *U-47* (Commanding Officer: Kapitänleutnant Prien) on October 14, 1939. Dr Mayer proves this with the facts that *U-47* fired torpedoes produced in pre-war time and that your findings show, among others, the following characteristics of pre-war production:

– Only torpedoes G7e have double-bladed propellers.

– The mark "BMAG/VLS" stands for: Berliner Maschinenbau Aktiengesellschaft vormals L. Schwarzkopf, which means the producer.

– The brass plates 2874 and 2597 belong to G7e torpedoes produced in pre-war time only.

There are further characteristics, but their listing would go too deep into technical details. However, they have been checked with original diagrams. Let me congratulate you on your finding, which has a historical meaning, too, as far as it might help to disprove doubts about the truth of Kapitänleutnant Prien's ship's log . . .

The torpedo parts were an unexpected bonus, but nobody I talked to knew anything about a dance or anything about a driver of a car on the shore . . .

I contacted a number of *Royal Oak* survivors and, through the 1939 *Navy List* and *Who's Who*, a number of officers who were serving aboard ships in Scapa Flow on the night *Royal Oak* was lost. The editors of *Navy News*, the Royal Marine newspaper *Globe and Sceptre* and the Gordon Highlanders' regimental publication were kind enough to publish letters asking for personal reminiscences, and Gerry Meyer, editor of *The Orcadian*, carried a letter asking specifically for any information about visibility in Scapa Flow on the night of October 13–14, 1939, and whether there had been a dance at St Mary's.

The first envelope I opened contained a note which read:

Dear Sir, In answer to your request in our local paper for the following information about the *Royal Oak* (14/10/39), as a garage proprietor I was driving a taxi and I dropped some young people at St Mary's dance hall about 12.20 a.m. As I made my way from the back of the village, I stopped the car and noticed my one masked headlamp was piercing its light into the waters of Kirk Sound. The tide was very high and it was bright moonlight,* so I switched off the headlight and, with only sidelights, I drove along at full speed until I got past the Radar station when it suddenly began to rain and became dark. I remember switching on the headlight and windscreen wipers. I arrived home at Kirkwall at 12.40 a.m. Yours truly, R. Tullock.

I caught the night sleeper to Inverness and the morning plane to Kirkwall.

---

* This was not the case.

Mr Tullock told his story in a perfectly straightforward manner, but it contained one puzzling feature. When I asked him why he had kept his identity secret all these years and never mentioned his trip to St Mary's to anyone outside his family, he replied that he did not think his experience was 'of any interest'. This was clearly evasive in view of the fact that, in the Orkneys, the loss of *Royal Oak* is as immediate as if the event happened yesterday, and his explanation made me inclined to think he might be volunteering for a place in history.

However, there was definitely a dance. On my first visit I had met James McDonald, a member of the maintenance staff at Kirkwall Hospital, who as a boy had helped to lay the blockship *Soriano* in Kirk Sound and later served on the Scapa Flow boom defences. It was his suggestion that the matter of the dance might be verified by consulting 'Jean Petrie at the electrician's. She lived in St Mary's in 1939 and was known as a great dancer.'

Miss Petrie said, yes, there had definitely been a dance but she, for once, had been unable to attend. 'I had been invited to a wedding on one of the islands,' she said. 'But I remember quite clearly missing the dance because of the wedding and that the wedding took place on the same day that the *Royal Oak* was sunk. Everybody was talking about it when I came home on the Saturday night.'

That still left the mystery of Mr Tullock's long silence. I eventually discovered Mr Willie Irving, the Water Board engineer in Kirkwall, a relation who was living with Mr Tullock in the autumn of 1939 because his own parents were abroad, and explained my difficulty. Did he remember when Mr Tullock had first mentioned his trip to St Mary's?

'The very next morning, as soon as we heard the news that the *Royal Oak* had been sunk,' he said. 'As for his silence, that's very simple. He didn't want to be involved – people are like that around here – and he was also afraid it might be suggested that his headlight helped the U-boat in some way. But his main concern was about the three soldiers at the door of the dance hall. He thought perhaps they should have been down by the shore and, if he came forward and told his story, they would get into trouble.'

That seemed an adequate explanation, and, of course, the map published subsequently in *The Royal Oak Disaster* confirmed the presence of three guards on the shore at the same time as the car.

The General Register and Record Office of Shipping and Seamen in Cardiff, part of the Department of Trade, produced the log and crew list of the *Bosnia* from which – another unexpected bonus – the General Council of British Shipping, which deals with Merchant Navy pensions, was able to provide the address of Mr Denis Bird.

Lt. Prien has been subjected to some criticism over an incident I have not dealt with in the main text – his claim to have torpedoed the cruiser HMS *Norfolk* on November 28, 1939. This claim was promptly inflated by the German Propaganda Ministry into a positive sinking.

Sir Winston Churchill recorded in *The Gathering Storm*, the first volume of his history of the second World War, that this claim caused 'lively distress' until it was proved to be false, and also quotes a description of the damage to *Norfolk*, taken from *U-47*'s log: 'The upper deck is buckled and torn. The starboard torpedo mounting is twisted backwards over the ship's side. The aircraft is resting on the tail unit.' The log of *Norfolk* carries the more laconic statement: '1340 Torpedo exploded port beam. Action stations.' and there is no mention of any damage.

However, after two days on patrol, the cruiser spent 12 days in Harland and Wolff's shipyard at Belfast. Her *Ship's Book*, still covered by the 30-year secrecy rule but produced by Mr Robin Little of Defence Secretariat 16, showed that *Norfolk*'s visit to Belfast had nothing to do with the torpedo attack. The work consisted of examining her keel for possible storm damage;

inspecting underwater fittings, which were found to be satisfactory; lightly welding or caulking some butts which were leaking; replacing some loose rivets in the forepeak; and testing one boiler.

Later it transpired that Lt. Prien had apparently once again been the victim of circumstances. A detailed report of the supposed damage to *Norfolk* is attached to the log of *U-47*, now back in Freiburg. It is signed by Lt. Endrass, who presumably made the observation, admittedly in atrocious weather conditions.

I must also thank Wren First Officer Jenny MacColl for information about how the Royal Navy recorded the weather in 1939; Lt.-Cdr. John Dempsey, RN, of HMS *Mercury* for details of visual signalling procedures in 1939; the Naval Historical Branch (Ministry of Defence); Mr Alex Bruce of the Commissioners for Northern Lighthouses for information about the switching on of lights during the war; Captain Ö. Dannevig Hauge, head of the Maritime Department of the Bergen Steamship Co., and Captain Fritjof Qvigstad, chief officer in 1939 of the steamship *Meteor* on the Bergen–Newcastle run; Messrs. Barr and Stroud Ltd. and Carl Zeiss (Oberkocken) for helpful information about binoculars; Alan Hedgeley, public affairs manager for Harland and Wolff, Belfast; the library staff at Lloyd's of London and Greenwich Maritime Museum; and Graham Griffin, a neighbour who served in the Royal Navy during the war, checked some of the navigation in this book and listened to most of the arguments.

Initially, I did not have much success with inquiries in Germany, perhaps understandably. Admiral Dönitz did not reply when I wrote to him. Gerhard Hänsel, one of two ratings on *U-47*'s bridge throughout the Scapa Flow action, did not reply when I wrote to him. Ernst Dziallas, the other rating, did answer, asking what struck me as a curious question: Did I want information out of private interest or for publication? I repeated what I thought I had already made quite clear, that the information was required for publication. I did not hear from Herr Dziallas again.

But things went rather better in the latter stages. Fräulein Christina Adlung of Verlag Ullstein was particularly helpful in answering preliminary questions about *Mein Weg Nach Scapa Flow* and putting me in touch with Herr Cyrill Soschka; and, when I ultimately went to West Berlin, the library staff of *Die Welt* were kind enough to make 'a special case' and allow me to read their cuttings on Paul Weymar.

The Bibliothek für Zeitgeschichte in Stuttgart made their contribution and the Bundesarchiv-Militärarchiv at Freiburg could not have been more co-operative, preparing a pile of relevant documents before my arrival with the result that research which might have taken days was completed in a matter of hours.

Finally, my most profound thanks are due to everyone quoted in the text. Perhaps I may be forgiven for selecting two of them for special mention – David Lees, always liberal with time and information, and kind enough to read the manuscript of this book before publication; and Lt. Prien's widow, Frau Sturm.

Before going to see her in Cologne, I asked if I might bring my 10-year-old son in order to disabuse him of the notion, gathered from TV, that everybody in Germany wears a long raincoat and carries a gun. She readily agreed. While we were having a drink before lunch, her present husband said: 'Excuse me a moment. I have something to show your son.'

He went away and came back a couple of minutes later wearing a long raincoat. Over each shoulder was slung a hunting rifle, and in his right hand he carried a Luger air pistol.

Appendix B

Flaws in the Scapa Defences

The *Royal Oak* Board of Inquiry listed the following 11 means by which a U-boat could have penetrated Scapa Flow on the night of October 13–14, 1939:

1)   Passing through the gap at the Flotta end of the Hoxa boom on the surface or trimmed down. This gap is (?) feet wide with a least depth of water of 15 feet at high water and considerably more over the greater part. There was no lookout on the shore at the gap. One drifter was pat rolling the whole entrance, which is one and a half miles wide. Approaching this gap would take the submarine within five cables of the battery on Stanger Head.
2)   Passing submerged through the gate in the Hoxa boom while it was opened to allow vessels to pass. No hydrophone or asdic watch is maintained at or inside the entrance when the gate is open. Entry here would be a difficult operation, but is possible.
3)   By passing under the Hoxa boom. The foot of the net at this boom is 25 feet above the sea bottom at low water and approximately 35 feet above the bottom at high water springs. In these circumstances we think it would be quite possible for a small submarine proceeding very close to or scraping the bottom to get through without much disturbing the boom.
4)   Passing through the gap at the Flotta end of Switha boom on the surface. There was no lookout on shore at this gap and no patrol vessel at the boom.
5)   Passing through the gap at the Hoy end of Hoy boom on the surface or trimmed down. This gap is 500 feet wide with a depth

of water of 30 feet. There was no lookout stationed on shore at this gap. One drifter was patrolling this boom, which, with the gap, is 1.7 miles long.

6)   Passing through the opening in Kirk Sound south of ss *Thames* on the surface. This opening is 400 feet wide with a depth of four to four and a half fathoms (24–27ft.) at low water. There is another opening about 200 feet wide with a depth of 15 feet or more at high water. Note: An additional blockship has been placed in this entrance since October 14.

7)   Passing through the opening in Skerry Sound on the surface. This opening is 240 feet wide with a depth of 15 feet or more at high water.

8)   Passing through the opening in East Weddell Sound on the surface. This opening is 460 feet wide with a depth of 15 feet or more at high water. The depth in the centre is three to four fathoms (18–24ft.) at low water.

9)   Passing through the openings in Water Sound on the surface. One of these openings is 400 feet wide and the other 200 feet wide. Both have a depth of 15 feet or more at high water.

No lookout is kept at any of the entrances on the east side of the Flow mentioned in 6, 7, 8 and 9 above.

Appendix C

The Admiral and the Bandmaster

The Royal Navy today is a vastly different organisation, not just in terms of size, from the Royal Navy of the inter-war years. Its spirit and attitudes half a century ago can perhaps best be captured by a brief outline of the events which took place aboard *Royal Oak* in the Grand Harbour at Malta on the night of January 12, 1928, and of the consequences which flowed from them.

It was the night of the wardroom dance. After dinner, the battleship's officers, their wives, their girlfriends and their guests began to drift up to the quarter-deck where Bandmaster Barnacle and his Marine musicians were already playing some of the latest American tunes beneath the striped awning and fairy lights. Among the early arrivals was Admiral Collard who, after promotion from Captain, had arrived in Malta just over two months earlier and hoisted his flag for the first time in *Royal Oak*. Admiral Collard was an officer of the old school, inclined to shortness of temper and abrasiveness of tongue, who had begun his naval career as a Midshipman under sail and had himself, when only a Lieutenant 20 years earlier, been the central figure in another celebrated naval court martial following the affair known as 'The Portsmouth Mutiny'.

On a November evening in 1905, while serving as the senior gunnery officer at R.N. Barracks, Portsmouth, he had ordered a sailor to kneel to be reprimanded after he had twice answered, 'Here', to his name instead of the regulation, 'Here, sir, please'. Various distorted versions of the story appeared in popular newspapers and contributed to some extent in creating the right climate for the dramatic happenings which took place precisely a year later.

Faced on this occasion by a group of disgruntled stokers on parade, Lt. Collard again gave the order: 'On the knee.' At first all refused, but eventually, with the exception of one man, they obeyed the command. After this capitulation, Lt. Collard dismissed them, had a private word with the dissident stoker, then dismissed him as well. This, it appeared, was the end of the incident, but that night, and again the next, rioting broke out in the barracks, bottles, glasses, windows and furniture were smashed, flower beds trampled on.

Once the root cause of this unheard-of indiscipline had been established, Lt. Collard was court-martialled and charged with giving an unauthorised punishment (ordering the first sailor to kneel to be reprimanded); using abusive language to a stoker; and making improper use of the order, 'On the knee', which, it seemed, was a long-established but little-used command, designed to enable an officer to see all the men he was addressing and the men to see him.

Lt. Collard received a sympathetic hearing, was found guilty of only one offence – giving an unauthorised punishment – and reprimanded. The incident did not mar his naval career, but it did substantially enrich his pocket. Edgar Wallace, sent to cover the case for a London newspaper, wrote: 'If men are treated like animals they will behave like animals . . . It is a significant fact that four years ago Lt. Collard was involved in a similar case, which resulted in a court of inquiry and in Lt. Collard losing six months' seniority.'

Lt. Collard's protests over this charge, which was untrue, led to his receiving a public apology and £5,000 from the newspaper concerned. In addition, Edgar Wallace was fired, although, in retrospect, this was not such a bad thing, for the loss of his newspaper job launched him on his highly successful career as a writer of thrillers.

As with the sinking in 1939, there are two contradictory

accounts of what happened aboard *Royal Oak* on the night of the 1928 wardroom dance and during its aftermath. One belongs to Admiral Collard, the other to two of the battleship's officers, Captain Kenneth Dewar, Flag-Captain of *Royal Oak*, and Commander Henry Daniel, *Royal Oak*'s Commander.

According to the two officers, the dancing had barely started when Admiral Collard buttonholed Captain Dewar and complained that too many of the feminine guests were sitting out instead of dancing. Captain Dewar took the matter up with the Commander, who reassured him that everything would be in order once the dance was properly under way and dance cards had been completed. This matter had not long been settled when Admiral Collard, by-passing his Flag-Captain, approached Commander Daniel directly and ordered him to replace the Marine band with the ship's jazz band.

Then, Commander Daniel later explained, when the band had finished a tune, Admiral Collard marched over and addressed himself to Bandmaster Barnacle. 'Come here, you,' he said. 'Stand here. You call yourself a flagship band? I never heard such a bloody awful noise in my life. Your playing is like a dirge and everybody is complaining. I'll have you sent home and reported to your headquarters.' In the stunned silence which followed this outburst, Admiral Collard turned away and was heard to say quite distinctly: 'I won't have a bugger like that on my ship.'

It is a tribute to the tact and persuasiveness of Commander Daniel that the jazz band was substituted for the Marine band without the vast majority of guests being aware of the reasons for the change. The matter was far from over, however. Next day, Bandmaster Barnacle announced that he wished to leave the Royal Marines; two members of his band asked to be drafted from the ship; and both Major Claude Attwood, the Major of Marines, and the Rev. Harry Goulding, *Royal Oak*'s chaplain, registered protests over the Admiral's 'insulting behaviour'. According to the two officers, Commander Daniel was eventually given *carte blanche* to smooth things over, starting by conveying an apology from the Admiral to Bandmaster Barnacle.

There was, without doubt, a lack of warmth and understanding in the relationship between Admiral Collard and Captain Dewar which manifested itself again less than 24 hours later. Captain Dewar, who had what were considered to be unconventional views about how naval battles should be fought, had spent much of the week demonstrating his theories in a war game involving two Fleets, one using accepted tactics, the other using the Captain's. At the finish on the Saturday, Admiral Collard, who had agreed to serve as referee, was so harshly critical of his Flag-Captain that Admiral Sir Roger Keyes, the Malta C.-in-C. who was present, later raised the matter with his depty, Vice-Admiral John Kelly, and asked him to establish that all was well aboard *Royal Oak*.

Captain Dewar stayed ashore on the Sunday and was not present when Admiral Collard dropped into the wardroom, by invitation, for a pre-lunch drink. It was a convivial occasion, according to Commander Daniel, and, when the Admiral was leaving, he stepped outside with him and conveyed the news that he had apologised to Bandmaster Barnacle, the apology had been accepted and the whole matter might be considered closed. The Admiral, he said, expressed his gratitude at having been extricated from 'a damned nasty hole'.

This was the beginning of a truce which lasted until March 5. *Royal Oak* returned to harbour that night after rough weather had put an end to gunnery practice and some genuine confusion seems to have arisen about Admiral Collard's plans. It was the Admiral's intention to leave the ship as soon as she anchored. He therefore asked for a gangway on the port side, which would at that time be the lee of *Royal Oak* and enable his barge to come alongside in sheltered water. Only part of this request reached Commander Daniel, however. Unaware that the Admiral intended to leave the ship so promptly, he had the gangway made ready on the starboard side, which would be the weather side of *Royal Oak* until she had swung round on her anchor.

This, according to Captain Dewar and his Commander, led to another unpleasant and embarrassing scene after which the Admiral, clearly in a filthy temper, stomped off the ship, hurling back another order as he left. He wanted Commander Daniel's 'reasons in writing' for failure to carry out instructions. The Admiral's mood did not seem to have changed for the better when he returned on board late the following afternoon. On reaching the head of the gangway he marched straight off to his cabin, totally ignoring the officers, including Captain Dewar, who had gathered to greet him.

If, in his 'reasons in writing', Commander Daniel had confined himself to an explanation of the muddle over the gangway, the incident would almost certainly have ended there. He was so aggrieved, however, that he also went over the scene at the dance and included the 'insult' offered by Admiral Collard when he failed to acknowledge the officers waiting to receive him on his return to the ship. All *Royal Oak*'s officers, he said, 'are deeply resentful of the humiliation to which they see their Captain and ship have been subjected'. Assurance was needed, he went on, that 'discipline, which must depend on respect for rank, will not be undermined in this way'. He ended with the provocative comment that the ship was 'discouraged' and her crew thought Admiral Collard would make a forthcoming inspection the occasion for 'vindictive fault-finding'. On reading this letter, Captain Dewar realised that it was dynamite. He suggested that parts of it might be toned down. Commander Daniel refused to make any changes. In the circumstances, Captain Dewar, still smarting himself over the two gangway incidents, decided the time had come for a showdown. He addressed his Commander's 'reasons in writing' to Admiral Kelly, the deputy C.-in-C., via Admiral Collard, and with them he sent a letter of his own which began: 'I am extremely loth to make a complaint against a senior officer, Rear-Admiral Bernard St George Collard, but I have no alternative as his behaviour is calculated to undermine not only my position but also the general discipline of the ship which I have the honour to command . . .'

Captain Dewar, too, described the dance incident . . . the subsequent apology to which the Admiral had agreed under pressure . . . the first gangway incident at which he, Dewar, had been subjected to 'a threatening and aggressive tirade, the main points of which were, a) he could not get a single order obeyed on the bloody ship, b) he was treated worse than a Midshipman, c) he would not stay in this rotten ship and would ask to have his flag shifted . . .' and the second gangway incident at which the Admiral's 'general attitude and demeanour had every appearance of a studied insult to me in the presence of a large number of officers and men'.

The two letters did not reach Admiral Kelly until the afternoon of Friday, March 9, just 24 hours before the Mediterranean Fleet was due to sail for joint exercises with the Atlantic Fleet. Admiral Kelly decided, not unwisely, that the matter was too hot for him to handle and passed the buck to Admiral Keyes. Never slow to act when action was required, the C.-in-C. decided at once that the three officers involved could not possibly sail in the same ship. He instructed Admiral Kelly to convene a court of inquiry for the following day and postponed the sailing of the Fleet.

The court of inquiry dragged on throughout the Saturday. Admiral Collard, given first say in the morning, denied that he had abused Bandmaster Barnacle or behaved unreasonably: Captain Dewar and Commander Daniel, interrogated in the afternoon and evening, insisted that he had. What concerned the court most, however, was not so much who had said what to whom but whether the Captain and his Commander had behaved improperly in forwarding their criticisms of a superior officer. The decision went against them. Soon after lunch on the Sunday they were summoned before Admiral Keyes and informed that they had been dismissed their ship. Captain Dewar promptly asked what offence he had committed to deserve such a harsh punishment and, when he received no satisfactory answer, announced that he would seek a court martial.

The Fleet finally sailed early on the Monday morning, more than 36 hours behind schedule. By then Captain Dewar and Commander Daniel were already on their way home to Britain. Admiral Collard did not sail with the Fleet either. He had decided voluntarily to strike his flag and leave *Royal Oak*. As it happened, he was never to serve in a ship of the Royal Navy again.

When Captain Dewar and his Commander reached London on Thursday, March 15, they were left to kick their heels. Nobody at the Admiralty was at that stage quite clear about what had actually happened. A wireless message sent by Admiral Keyes had become garbled in transmission and the courier carrying his full written report had not yet arrived. A brief news agency message from Malta, however, had been published and, when this was made the subject of a question in the House of Commons late on the Thursday, the newspapers at once sniffed a naval scandal.

MUTINY AT MALTA . . . NAVAL OFFICERS REBEL . . . TROUBLE IN *ROYAL OAK* – the Friday papers were full of the story. Reporters were despatched by car, boat and train to Gibraltar where the Mediterranean Fleet had berthed after its exercises. Others besieged the Admiralty once it was learned that two of the officers intimately involved had reached London. The courier also arrived bearing Admiral Keyes's report, which included the warning that Captain Dewar and Commander Daniel might do precisely what they were at that moment doing – trying to arrange court martials for themselves.

Admiral Keyes suggested that to grant such requests would be unwise because of 'the inevitable publicity it would attract'. By this time, however, William Bridgeman, the First Lord of the Admiralty, was in no mood to listen to advice from Admiral Keyes. The newspapers were after blood, the House of Com-

mons was after blood, and even King George V had expressed
his personal concern over what was happening in, and being said
about, his Navy.

When the First Lord rose to make his promised statement in
the Commons on the Monday, he announced that 'certain issues
important from a discipline point of view' were to be examined
by courts martial. Captain Dewar and Commander Daniel had
been given what they wanted and the First Lord had taken
much of the pressure off himself. In the face of any awkward
questions, he – and, for that matter, anyone else in authority –
could refuse legitimately to answer on the grounds that the case
was now *sub judice*.

At the Admiralty 24 hours later, Captain Dewar and Commander Daniel were handed copies of the charges they were to
face. There were two – writing *and* forwarding subversive
documents. Both protested at once that the charges were too
vague, and Captain Dewar made a written request that they
should either be broadened, or made more precise, to give him
an opportunity to raise the matter of Admiral Collard's previous
conduct. This plea was rejected. The Admiralty did, however,
agree to make Admiral Collard available as a witness for the
prosecution, which would give the defence a chance 'of eliciting
such facts as they may think necessary'.

By this time, the Admiral had been sent home on leave and
placed on half pay. He had, however, barely arrived at the house
in Surrey which he had built with the £5,000 from the Edgar
Wallace case when he was ordered to proceed to Gibraltar.
There, on the morning of Saturday, March 31, the court martial
of Commander Daniel opened in the main hangar of the aircraft
carrier HMS *Eagle*.

The start had been delayed for 24 hours because the Commander now faced two additional charges, added at the last
minute – making public the contents of each of the two
controversial letters by reading parts of them to fellow-officers
in *Royal Oak*. Commander Daniel pleaded not guilty to these

allegations as well as to the original charges of writing and forwarding subversive documents.

Once the hearing began, Admiral Collard gave for the first time in public his version of what had happened at the momentous dance 11 weeks earlier. Captain Dewar had appeared angry when the matter of the wallflowers was raised. The Admiral had decided, however, not to make an issue of this reaction and had simply commented: 'Better make the Commander do his job.' Admiral Collard agreed that he had found the music dreary and impossible to dance to, but his version of the conversation with Bandmaster Barnacle was quite different from the recollections of Captain Dewar and Commander Daniel. He had eventually gone up to Mr Barnacle and said: 'Bandmaster, what is the matter with the music? I don't think I ever heard such a bloody awful noise in my life.' Bandmaster Barnacle had replied: 'I'm sorry, sir, I shall try to do better.' As they walked away, the Admiral had said to Commander Daniel, not loud enough for the Bandmaster to hear: 'I can't have a bloody man like that in the flagship. I must get rid of him.'

Admiral Collard denied that he had authorised the Commander to apologise on his behalf; or that he had referred to Bandmaster Barnacle as 'a bugger'; or that he had thanked Commander Daniel for extricating him from 'a damned nasty hole'. The first gangway incident? On that occasion it had been Captain Dewar who lost his temper. 'I then turned to him and said I was sick of him as Flag-Captain,' the Admiral explained. 'Either he would have to go or I would have to shift my flag.' As for the 'studied insult' incident, on coming aboard, he said, he had saluted the quarter deck 'in the usual way'.

When called to give evidence on the Monday, Commander Daniel was asked why he had written his letter. 'I felt that unless there could be a total stoppage of such incidents there was no chance of preserving the morale of the ship,' he explained. 'I was very reluctant to write it in view of my pleasant personal relationship with the Admiral.'

His reasons for 'publishing' the two letters were straightforward. He had gone over some aspects of his own letter with fellow-officers in order to satisfy himself that what he was saying was absolutely true. Captain Dewar's letter had been read in the scramble to obtain witnesses for the hurriedly convened Malta court of inquiry. After stressing the main points at issue, he had asked anyone 'who had the guts' to attend the hearing and give evidence.

Under cross-examination by the prosecution, however, Commander Daniel was forced to make some unfortunate admissions. He agreed that his letter had been 'rather peculiar' and, in introducing the dance incident when asked to explain the first gangway incident, he had exceeded his orders and created a situation which made it impossible for him and the Admiral to continue to serve in the same ship. Asked whether the suggestion that Admiral Collard would use the ship's inspection as an occasion for 'vindictive fault-finding' was 'a proper statement to make about a senior officer', Commander Daniel replied somewhat unconvincingly: 'I submit it is another way of saying the Admiral had a down on the ship.'

The evidence of several defence witnesses, including Captain Dewar, suggested that Admiral Collard's recollection of events was less than accurate. Major Attwood, for example, spoke of hearing 'raised, angry voices' at the dance and he had also observed 'Admiral Collard shaking his fist at the Bandmaster'. It was only the Major's prompt action in obtaining an apology for the Bandmaster and his men which had avoided trouble in the ship.

The prosecution's main point at the summing-up, however, was that Commander Daniel's letter was subversive by its very nature, no matter where the truth lay about the facts on which it was based. In addition, allegations that the events described had had a bad effect on morale and discipline were only 'vague'. It was an argument which the court accepted. Commander Daniel returned to his sword pointing towards him. Found guilty of all four charges, he was ordered to be dismissed his ship – at the time, HMS *Cormorant*, the shore base at Gibraltar, to which he had been attached for the court martial – and severely reprimanded.

Captain Dewar, in turn, pleaded not guilty to the two charges against him when his case began on Wednesday, April 4.

His questioning of Admiral Collard, while producing some brisk exchanges, did nothing to shake the Admiral's story. Subsequently, however, he scored a telling point when he examined Admiral Kelly about what he had done with the two letters when they reached him.

'I took them to the Commander-in-Chief,' he replied.

'Why?'

'Because I thought there was no other course open to me.'

Captain Dewar thanked him politely for the admission which, in effect, meant that, if the Captain was guilty of forwarding a subversive document, so was the Admiral.

Later, when himself questioned again, Captain Dewar said he blamed 'uncontrollable fits of temper on the part of Admiral Collard', for all the trouble in *Royal Oak*. Why had he not talked the matter over with the Admiral? 'I felt any personal protest would have been ineffectual. Admiral Collard would have immediately lost his temper and threatened me with a court martial.'

In his address to the court, Captain Dewar said: 'I treated Admiral Collard as an honoured guest of the ship. But how could I hope to maintain my authority if he attacked me in this way? Being convinced these incidents had to stop, what was I to do? If I went to him I knew I should be bullied. I might have gone privately to the Vice-Admiral, but I do not believe in creeping up back stairs . . .

'It was I who pressed for a court martial and a broad charge . . . I am now before you on the trivial charge of having failed sufficiently to censor a letter . . . I submit there is absolutely no case against me . . . A great question of justice and principle is involved. I ask the court not only to acquit me, but to acquit me honourably . . .'

The final argument put forward by the prosecution was basically that Captain Dewar had not made proper use of the 'reasons in writing' procedure, which was designed for 'the avoidance of heated discussion, to give the junior an opportunity for explanation and the senior a chance to consider that explanation when the heat of the moment had passed.' 'I submit,' said the prosecutor, 'that anyone who had the welfare of the Service at heart would have restrained himself a little longer, and forwarded a proper letter of "reasons in writing", and quietly made known his own cause of complaint at a later and more convenient date.'

It took the court only 20 minutes to come to the conclusion that Captain Dewar was guilty of only one offence – forwarding Commander Daniel's subversive letter. He, too, was dismissed his ship and severely reprimanded, and a subsequent appeal failed to upset the sentence. That was, however, by no means the end of the affair. The rights and wrongs of the case continued to be debated both in Parliament and the newspapers with all three parties to the action – Admiral Collard, the two court-martialled officers and the Admiralty – having their champions and critics.

One general cause for concern was that neither Captain Dewar nor Commander Daniel should have their naval careers ruined for having committed a technical offence arising from a clash of personalities. But, in the end, neither they nor Admiral Collard escaped unscathed.

Immediately after the courts martial, the Admiral was placed on the retired list, the First Lord explaining in a statement to the Commons that 'he had dealt with trivial causes for dissatisfaction in a manner unbecoming his position and showed himself unfitted to hold further high command . . .' The decision meant that he missed the knighthood which, in the normal course of events, would almost certainly have been his as a matter of routine.

Commander Daniel, feeling that he would be a marked man henceforth, resigned from the Royal Navy almost at once and joined the *Daily Mail* as its naval correspondent. He was not temperamentally suited, however, to the hustle and bustle of Fleet Street and resigned in 1931 to devote himself to freelance writing. That did not prove a success and he drifted from one job to another. Eventually his health broke down and he died from arterio-sclerosis in South Africa in 1955.

Captain Dewar, contrary to the betting, was given a new command, HMS *Tiger*, an elderly battlecruiser. This appointment enabled him to complete the sea-time he needed to qualify for promotion, but as soon as he was made up to Rear-Admiral in 1929 he was placed on the retired list. He wrote a book called *The Navy From Within*; returned to a desk job during the second World War; and afterwards became an intermittent writer of letters to the newspapers on naval topics.

In his full-length book *The Royal Oak Courts Martial* author Leslie Gardiner makes one interesting point which will appeal to collectors of coincidences. He says: 'Collard's name and Dewar's, bracketed together so many times in the Press in the spring of 1928, were bracketed again, and for the last time' in the spring of 1962. 'On the correspondence page of *The Times* appeared, as its principal letter of the day, a warning to the Government by Admiral Dewar regarding the proposal to spend twenty million pounds on a Polaris submarine. Opposite, Admiral Collard's death was announced, at the age of eighty-six.'

The date was Friday, April 13.

Datum und Uhrzeit	Angabe des Ortes, Wind, Wetter, Seegang, Beleuchtung, Sichtigkeit der Luft, Mondschein usw.	Vorkommnisse
12.10.39	SO 7 - 6, bedeckt.	Östlich der Orkneys tagsüber auf Grund gelegen. Abends aufgetaucht und zur Feststellung des Schiffsortes auf die Küste zugelaufen. Von 2200 bis 2230 Uhr sind die Engländer so freundlich, mir die gesamte Küstenbefeuerung einzuschalten, sodaß ich genauesten Schiffsort bekomme ! Obwohl seit Auslaufen aus Weg I keine Besteckmöglichkeit mehr bestand, sodaß nur nach Koppelung und Lotung gefahren wurde, stimmte der Schiffsort auf 1,8 sm.
13.10.39	Östlich Orkney Inseln. NNO 3 - 4, leicht bewölkt, sehr helle Nacht, Nordlicht am ganzen Nordhorizont.	Um 0437 Uhr Boot auf 90 m Wasser auf Grund gelegt. Ruhe für die Besatzung. Um 1600 Uhr allgemeines Wecken. Nach dem Frühstück um 1700 Uhr Vorbereitungen zum Angriff auf Scapa Flow. Es werden 2 Torpedos in Schnelladestellung vor Rohr I und II gebracht. Im Boot Sprengkörper ausgebracht für den Fall der Sprengung. Stimmung in der Besatzung ist hervorragend. Um 1915 Uhr aufgetaucht. Nach einem warmen Abendessen für die ganze Besatzung Marsch nach Holm Sound angetreten. Alles geht planmäßig bis 2307 Uhr kurz vor Rose Ness vor einem Dampfer getaucht werden muß. Trotz der sehr hellen Nacht und der brennenden Lichter kann ich den Dampfer in keinem der beiden Sehrohre ausmachen. Um 2331 Uhr wieder aufgetaucht und in den Holm Sound eingelaufen. Einlaufender Strom. Bei
	Die Sicht ist ganz übel. Unter Land ist alles dunkel, hoch am Himmel ist das flackernde Nordlicht, sodaß die Bucht, die von ziemlich hohen Bergen umgeben ist, direkt von oben beleuchtet wird. Gespenstisch wie Theaterkulissen stehen	Näherkommen ist der im Skerry-Sound versenkte Dampfer sehr gut zu sehen, sodaß ich zunächst glaube, schon im Kirk-Sound zu stehen und daraufzulaufe. Der Obersteuermann stellt aber anhand seiner Koppelung das zu frühe Andrehen fest, während ich aber gleichzeitig den Fehler erkenne, weil nur ein Dampfer in der Enge versenkt liegt. Durch hartes Abdrehen nach St.B. kann die bestehende Gefahr beseitigt werden. Wenige Augenblicke später ist der Kirk-Sound frei einzusehen. Es bewahrheitet sich jetzt, daß ich die Karte vorher auswendig gelernt habe, denn die Durchfahrt geht mit unglaublicher Geschwindigkeit vor sich. Ich hatte mich inzwischen entschlossen, im Norden die Sperrschiffe zu passieren. Mit 270° wird der Zweimastschoner, der mit Kurs 315° vor der eigentlichen Sperre liegt, auf 15 m Abstand

Following German routine, the handwritten log of the *U-47* was typed and copies sent to the Commanding Officers concerned. The three pages covering the Scapa Flow action are reproduced here.

Datum und Uhrzeit	Angabe des Ortes, Wind, Wetter, Seegang, Beleuchtung, Sichtigkeit der Luft, Mondschein usw.	Vorkommnisse
10.39	die Sperrschiffe in den Sunden.	passiert. Im nächsten Augenblick wird das Boot vom Strom erfaßt und nach St.B. gedreht. Gleichzeitig wird die in Winkel von 45° nach vorn zeigende Ankerkette des nördlichen Sperrschiffes erkannt. Mit B.B.-Maschine Stopp, St.B.-Maschine langsam voraus und hart B.B. Ruder dreht das Boot zunächst sehr langsam, berührt Grund. Die vorgefluteten Tauchbunker und Zellen werden ausgeblasen, das Boot dreht, dreht weiter. Das Heck berührt noch die Ankerkette, Boot ist frei, wird nach B.B. herumgerissen und läßt sich nur mit harten schnellen Maßnahmen wieder auf Kurs bringen, aber:
10.39 27		Wir sind in Scapa Flow !!!

Es ist unförderlich hell. Die ganze Bucht ist fabelhaft zu übersehen. Südlich Cava liegt nichts. Ich laufe noch näher. Da erkenne ich an B.B. die Hoxa-Sound Bewachung, für die das Boot als Zielscheibe in den nächsten Sekunden erscheinen muß. Damit wäre alles umsonst, zumal sich südlich Cava noch immer keine Schiffe ausmachen lassen, obwohl sonst auf weiteste Entfernung alles klar erkennbar ist. |
55?		Also Entschluß: Südlich Cava liegt nichts, deshalb, bevor jede Aussicht auf Erfolg aufs Spiel gesetzt wird, müssen erreichbare Erfolge durchgeführt werden. Dementsprechend nach B.B. Kehrt gemacht. Unter der Küste nach Norden gelaufen. Dort liegen zwei Schlachtschiffe, weiter unter Land Zerstörer vor Anker. Kreuzer nicht auszumachen, Angriff auf die beiden dicken. Abstand 3 000 m. Ein-
16?	Nach Kriegskarte: 00.58 T (Repulse : Lords), T (Royal Oak)	gestellte Tiefe 7,5 m. Aufschlagzündung. Ein Schuß auf den nördlichen, zwei Schuß auf den südlich liegenden losgemacht. Es detoniert nach gut 3 1/2 Minuten ein Torpedo auf dem nördlich liegenden Schlachtschiff, von den anderen beiden ist nichts zu sehen ! Kehrt !
21? 25	Nach 01.02 Uhr 01.22	Heckschuß . im Bugraum zwei Rohre nachgeladen, rum ! 3 Bugschüsse. Nach je knappen 3 Minuten nach dem Abschüssen die Detonationen auf dem näherliegenden Schiff. Da rollt, knallt, bumst und grummelt es gewaltig. Zunächst Wassersäulen, dann Feuersäulen, Brocken fliegen durch die Luft. Jetzt wird es im Hafen lebendig, Zerstörer haben Lichter, aus allen Ecken wird gemorst, an Land, etwa 200 m von mir ab, brausen Autos über die Straßen. Es ist ein Schlachtschiff versenkt, ein weiteres beschädigt und drei Aale hat der Teufel geholt. Alle Rohre sind leer geschossen. Ich entschließe mich zum Auslaufen, denn: 1.) Getauchte Angriffe kann ich mit meinen Sehrohren nachts nicht fahren, siehe Einlauferfahrung.

B. 36.   Kriegstagebuch.   Din A 3

Datum und Uhrzeit	Angabe des Ortes, Wind, Wetter, Seegang, Beleuchtung, Sichtigkeit der Luft, Mondschein usw.	Vorkommnisse

14.10.39

lauferfahrung.
2.) Bei der hellen Nacht kann ich mich bei
   dem stillen Wasserspiegel nirgends ungesehen mehr hinbewegen.
3.) Ich muß annehmen, daß mich ein Autofahrer gesehen hat, der querab von uns
   stehen blieb, kehrt machte und mit hoher Fahrt nach Scapa zu wegfuhr.
4.) Weiter nach Norden kann ich auch nicht,
   denn dort liegen, gut gedeckt gegen
   Sicht durch mich schwach erkannten Zerstörer unter Land.

0128

Mit 2 x H.F.V. auf Auslaufkurs gegangen.
Zunächst ist bis Skildanoy Pt. alles einfach. Danach geht es wieder los. Der Wasserstand ist gefallen, einlaufender Strom.
Mit "L.F." und "K.F." versuche ich raus-
zukommen. Ich muß im Süden durch die Enge
wegen der Wassertiefe. Es geht die Irbe-
lei wieder los. Mit Kurs 58° und "L.F." =
10 sm stehe ich auf der Stelle. Mit "H.F."
dem südlichen Sperrschiff vorbeigequält.
Der Rudergänger arbeitet vorzüglich. Mit
2 x "H.F.", zuletzt mit "G.F." und "A.JV."
frei von der Schiffssperre, vor mir eine
Mole ! Mit harten Rudermanövern auch da
noch rum und um 0215 Uhr sind wir wieder
draußen. Schade, daß nur einer verrichtet
wurde.
   Die Torpedoversager erkläre ich mir
als entweder Geradlaufversager oder Ge-
schwindigkeitsfehler oder Absacker. Im
Rohr IV ein Rohrläufer.
   Bei der Unternehmung hat sich die Be-
satzung ganz ausgezeichnet bewährt. Am
13.10. morgens wurde im Schmieröl Wasser
(7 - 8%) festgestellt. In fieberhafter
Arbeit hat alles zugepackt, das Öl auszu-
wechseln, bzw. zu entwässern, und die
Leckstelle zu isolieren. - Das Torpedoper-
sonal hat mit bemerkenswerter Geschwin-
digkeit die Rohre nachgeladen. Das Boot
war so in Form, daß ich es mir leisten
konnte, im Hafen Ladung einzuschalten und
Luft aufzupumpen.

0215

Mit südöstlichen Kursen abgelaufen zum
Rückmarsch. Ich habe noch 5 Torpedos für
evtl. Handelskrieg.

0630 φ = 57° 58' N η = 1° 03' W

Auf Grund gelegt. Der Lichtschein von
Scapa ist noch lange zu sehen, anscheinend werfen sie noch Wasserbomben.

1935   ONO 3 - 4, leicht be-
wölkt, einzelne Re-
genschauer, Sicht
nach Land zu schlecht,
sonst gut.

Mit Kurs 180° weitergelaufen. Dieser
Kurs wird gewählt in der Hoffnung, viel-
leicht noch einen zu erwischen unter der
Küste und um "U 20" auszuweichen.

Prien

BIRLINN LTD (incorporating John Donald and Polygon) is one of Scotland's leading publishers with over four hundred titles in print. Should you wish to be put on our catalogue mailing list **contact**:

Catalogue Request
Birlinn Ltd
West Newington House
10 Newington Road
Edinburgh EH9 1QS
Scotland, UK

Tel: + 44 (0) 131 668 4371
Fax: + 44 (0) 131 668 4466
e-mail: info@birlinn.co.uk

Postage and packing is free within the UK. For overseas orders, postage and packing (airmail) will be charged at 30% of the total order value.

For more information, or to order online, visit our website at **www.birlinn.co.uk**

Birlinn *Limited*
Other Imprints – JOHN DONALD · POLYGON